THE MIND RULES

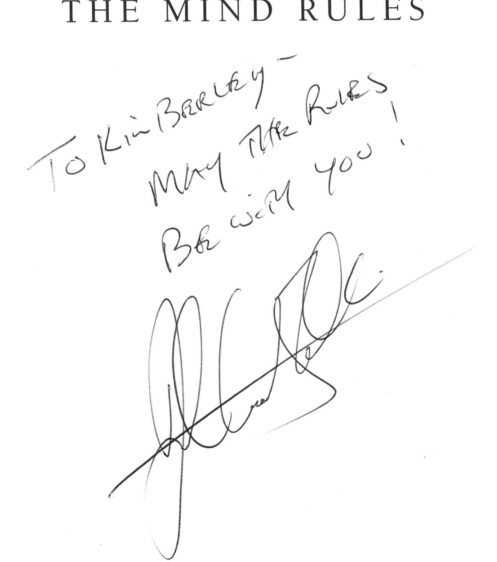

To Kimberley —
May The Rules
Be with you !

Real People, Real Challenges, Remarkable Solutions

"Sidelined from the running circuit for several years due to injury and turning forty did nothing for building my confidence when I decided to return to racing. With John's help, I surprised myself and surpassed my wildest expectations by posting a personal lifetime record in the San Diego Marathon. As a life-long competitive runner, beating my best was just too amazing."

ARDY JANKU, PILATES INSTRUCTOR,
OWNER: ARDY'S FITNESS TRAINING, RUNNER

"My husband Billy was a Superior Court Judge at the time of his stroke. He was forced to retire because he could no longer read, write, or talk. We had tried many forms of therapy, but Billy still had paralysis in his right side and was unable to communicate. Worse, Billy didn't like to be around his friends or others because he had no real speech and I had to talk for him. It hurt to see such a proud and brilliant man standing in the background.

"The weekend after our first visit with John, Billy and I went to a party. Before I knew what was happening, Billy was mixing in with the group and communicating! That Sunday, Billy picked out his best suit to wear to church and I knew that my husband's confidence was back. Best of all, that Thanksgiving, it was Billy who said grace at the dinner table. Our contact with John was one of the greatest things that has ever happened to us."

RUBYE MILLS, EDUCATOR, MOTHER

BILLY MILLS, SUPERIOR COURT JUDGE (RET.),
AUTHOR, COUNCILMAN CITY OF LOS ANGLES

"At thirty-two, I decided to go back to college and finish getting my degree. I was never an average student, I was barely a below-average student. At nineteen, I was told by an educator that I should find a different path through life, because for me to get a college degree would 'take a miracle.' Working with John Zulli was that miracle. John helped me rid my Subconscious of its old associations about school and taught me to use my mind in order to function at a college level. When we started, I felt that I did not have the mind power to memorize, comprehend, and articulate my thoughts well enough to graduate. When we finished, I not only realized that I can memorize, comprehend, and articulate my thoughts, but I pulled straight A's at one of the top universities in the nation. *The Mind Rules* is a must read for anyone who feels that they cannot accomplish a task or goal. *The Mind Rules* helped me to see myself as capable and then gave me the tools I needed to reach my goal. As a coach, I urge all who come in contact with this book to live the techniques that *The Mind Rules* teaches."

DAVID DEATON, SOCCER COACH, STUDENT, ATHLETE

"Stress is part of the territory when you are a business owner and mother. So when I started to have trouble sleeping, I wanted to do something about it but I didn't want to take medications. John taught me how to get my mind and body to work together and in no time I was getting a full evening of quality rest, every evening. But that's not all. Impressed with my success, I had John come in and teach The Mind Rules to our sales staff. Our sales numbers went through the roof and stayed there even in our slowest months! John Zulli is my secret weapon in the battle to stay number one in a highly competitive retail environment."

NOREEN MARTIN, CEO, A&R FURNITURE STORES, MOTHER

"After breaking my back, eye-socket, ribs, and skull in a serious motor-vehicle crash with a drunk driver, my performing career was at a stand-still. With the skills and training I learned from John, I recovered naturally, controlling my pain without medication. I bounced back to performing in an astonishing recovery time, and now speak to students worldwide about alcohol awareness and road safety. My confidence and knowledge in teaching and entertaining and my expertise in the field of helping people is credited to a man I consider one of the most influential human beings I have ever encountered."

MARC SAVARD, CHT, ENTERTAINER, EDUCATOR, AND SPEAKER

"John Zulli was instrumental in helping me to break free from old belief systems and take my success to the next level. The tools I learned from John gave me the confidence to open my own interior design studio. It is an amazing thing to realize that 'Yes I can,' after a lifetime of hearing that little voice that tells you otherwise. I still continue to use his tapes and teachings to motivate myself or over-come stressful times."

JULES DUROCHER, ASID, OWNER: DUROCHER DESIGN

"Just four days after our first meeting, I shot the best score I had posted in five months. Next week I play for the Club Championship and I have never felt more ready! This is a truly remarkable change with dramatic results."

RICHARD FOSTER, AMATEUR GOLFER

THE MIND RULES

Master the 3 powerful principles
that *rule* your performance,
success, and happiness

JOHN A. ZULLI

RED HORSE
PRESS

Red Horse Press, Inc. • San Luis Obispo, CA

Red Horse Press, Inc., P.O. Box 14609, San Luis Obispo, CA 93406-4609

ISBN 0-9752867-0-6

First Printing, October 2004

ACKNOWLEDGEMENTS

I could fill a book with the names of all the people who helped make this one a reality. This volume of acknowledgments would include every client I have worked with, teacher I have ever had, or book I have ever read, because each and every one pointed me toward the Rules. However, I'll spare you and limit myself to the short list of individuals who were essential to the creation of this book.

First, I am grateful to my three original teachers: Mark Gilboyne for his penetrating insight into human nature and his unfailing courage as a therapist and educator; John Kappas, Ph.D., for his understandable models of the mind and for teaching me how to hypnotize virtually anyone, and Ormond McGill for opening my eyes to the greatest gifts that come from trance.

Second, I am forever indebted to four men, not just for what they taught but also for the standards they set and examples they are: Mel Edelhertz, Robert Morales, Michael McMahon and Sam Trapasso.

Third, my most heartfelt gratitude to the people who stepped up to the plate when they were needed most: Art Horn, Rhonda Norton, Mark and Peggy Echart, Annelise Gerry, Carol Grant, and my favorite Martin.

Fourth, I want to thank the people who were directly involved in the development and preparation of *The Mind Rules*: Gary Holmes, Sallie Mitchell, Irene Rush, Maia Wilkinson, Julia Hing, Aimee West, Lisa Thomas, Ally Peltier, Jim Little, and Mary Lou Johnson. I especially want to thank my developmental editor Wendy Deaton, for her wisdom, enthusiasm, and support. This book is a better product by far because of her participation.

To my father for showing me the power of the spoken word,
and to my mother, whose laughter I can still hear.

TABLE *of* CONTENTS

RULE THREE THE RULE OF POWER

INTRODUCTION

This Is Your Brain on Life

Mrs. Janet Salas had a problem. She was pregnant, allergic to anesthesia, and needed to deliver her child by Cesarean Section. Janet's only defense against the pain would be her brain. In a film of the operation, Mrs. Salas is seen singing a hymn while surgeons slice through her side and remove her baby boy from her abdomen. In an interview following the birth, Mrs. Salas gives the doctors a play-by-play description of what took place in the operating room and tells them that she experienced absolutely no discomfort. Janet will go on to have two more children by the same method, using only her mind to control the pain. How is it that an average housewife from Michigan can harness powers that seem more at home in the hands of Indian gurus and martial art legends? Janet Salas was working with the Mind Rules.

Flash forward to the 1980's and television talk show goddess Oprah Winfrey. Fighting her personal battle of the bulge, Oprah went to a hypnotist who told her, "You will not eat French fries. You will not eat French fries." As soon as her session ended, Oprah walked out the door and immediately went and ate French fries. What caused Oprah to stumble so quickly? The hypnotist's poorly worded suggestions had set Oprah working in opposition to the Mind Rules.

That massive organ between your ears can sure seem fickle. One minute the mind is powerful enough to provide miraculous pain relief and the next minute it is too weak to stand up to a piece of chocolate cheesecake.

More than half a century has passed since Hans Selye's revolutionary stress research demolished the theory that the mind has little or no effect on the body. Yet, here in the Information Age, people seem utterly clueless when it comes to reaping tangible benefits from this mysterious connection. While we may admire the mental toughness of athletes and leaders, few Americans understand what mind power is, let alone how to put it to work healing their bodies, achieving their dreams, or finding that fundamental satisfaction that makes life worth living.

The Mind Rules takes the mystery out of getting your mind to mind and your body to behave. In three clear and powerful maxims, *The Mind Rules* helps you harness the essential skills of life-mastery: mental focus and discipline, deep personal transformation, and access to all the power, strength, and energy within you. The Rules are the foundation principles, guiding precepts, and active ingredients that make self-mastery and liberation possible. The Rules are like the constellations; you can navigate by them.

How can I be so sure that about these Rules and what they will do for you? For almost twenty years, I have used the Rules to help marathon runners move faster, children to stop wetting the bed, CEOs and single moms to deal better with high-pressure stress, and professionals in almost every field and art form to ramp up their performance and produce. I was there when the Mind Rules helped a rodeo rider earn a first-place trophy and when they gave a 93-year-old woman recovering from a broken hip the courage to face her pain and fear and learn to walk again. I have taught entire teams and organizations how to put these principles to use and, in *every* case, there was an improvement in production, an upwelling of morale, or a cut in cost such as workers compensation. In the last two decades, in thousands of sessions dealing with hundreds of issues, I have been privileged to watch as the Mind Rules pulled people through and created champions. The Rules have a proven track record and now I want to share these important precepts with you.

Another reason that the Mind Rules work is that they are ancient wisdom based in the bedrock of reality. I didn't invent these invaluable mind-body maxims. I inherited them. The Rules were distilled by some of the great original thinkers of the past and have recently been validated by the brilliant science of the present. The Rules are why athletes or cancer patients reap results from visualization exercises, and traces of these fundamental concepts can be found in every system of self-help, higher performance, or spiritual development. The Rules give martial artists their legendary power, and they form the foundations of some of the world's most practical and profound teachings. My contribution has been to take this important information and make it accessible and viable to the people who call the new millennium home.

I have written you a "self-help" book that I believe you will have a hard time putting down. The chapters are short and move directly to the heart of the matter. Most chapters start with a story, metaphor, or exercise that relates to the teaching tutorial that comes at the end. To keep things moving and not bog you down, I have eliminated a rehashing of old, tired background information and jettisoned most of the scientific jargon and references to research studies. My intent is to help you to achieve measurable success and personal triumph, not give you a science lesson.

Each Mind Rule also comes equipped with a set of exercises that teach you to apply these mind/body principles in real time and as you go about your busy day. Working with thousands of people in seminars and private sessions has made one thing clear—practicing the exercises is the weak point in almost everyone's personal growth or performance improvement program. To counter this deficit, I have crafted the majority of the Mind Rules exercises with your comfort and convenience in mind. Since you take your brain and body with you wherever you go, most of the exercises are designed to be practiced and utilized while you are engaged in living, working, or playing. You don't have to practice all these internal processes, but integrate a few of these mind/body workouts into your everyday world and just watch what happens to you.

Overall, my in goal in writing *The Mind Rules* has been to give you an experience. I want you to learn with all of your brain and as much of your body as possible. Through this intimate experience, the veil of mystery surrounding the mind and body connection is lifted and you harness this natural, internal power automatically and in your own unique way. The Rules are alive and at work within you. My hope is that the inspiring stories, tangible techniques, and straight talk you find in this book help you to recognize the power of the Rules and enable you to put them to good use.

Ready or not, crisis and opportunity are coming your way and they are traveling at light speed. *The Mind Rules* points the way to the well-head of inner resource and shows you how to meet any challenge focused, composed, and brimming with energy. You can live, work, and compete this way, every day...if you know the Rules.

RULE

THE RULE *of* PERFORMANCE

*"Where the mind goes,
the body and emotions follow"*

Welcome to Zoneville

CHAPTER | 1

When I was eight years old, I became an addict. As these things often happen, I got my first "taste" while playing with a group of friends behind the elementary school. The snow plow had cleared the parking lot and left a nine-foot-high mountain of white fluff that was a perfect battleground for a game of "king of the hill." As I stood at the base of the snow pile, preparing to attack, a wonderful feeling came over me. All at once I was joyful, energized, and intensely focused. My charge up the hill was a blur of snow pants and mittens, and I toppled the current king effortlessly!

For the next few minutes, I defended my mountain throne from a mob of determined boys with the grace and power of a pint-sized, kung fu monk. If they grabbed me, I slipped loose. If they went to push or strike, I was not there. When they attacked as a group, I became a whirling storm easily tossing four or five opponents down the hill as if they were nothing more than empty snowsuits. When the battle ended, I alone stood on the mountaintop with my exhausted foes sprawled about its base. But my victory was secondary to the magnificence of the *experience* itself. It was my first, memorable "peak experience" and I was hooked.

Today we have a name for this amazing state of unbreakable mental focus, remarkable physical power, and unshakable emotional composure: We call it the "zone." Finding the fabled zone, however, can be more elusive than sighting Elvis. Even the most gifted players have to go to great lengths to get its zip code. Golf great Tiger Woods learned to transform mind power into superior firepower with the help of psychologist Jay Brunza. Brunza taught the then thirteen-year-old Woods how to use hypnosis as a tool to self-induce this special mind/body state. Beyond elite athletes or serious king-of-the-hill competitors searching for the zone experience, business leaders, moms, and students are all finding that life is better in an ideal performance state. At high-end mind-body boot camps around the country, flabby Fortune 500 executives, hard-bodied housewives, and ten-year-old tennis stars on their way to Wimbledon fork over as much as $4,000 for a three-day program designed to sharpen their mental edge. Think four grand a little steep for a weekend seminar? One year of personal, "peak state" training with master motivator Tony Robbins can cost you $1,000,000.

The zone is obviously some very desirable real estate. However, you don't have to travel far to find your pathway to ideal performance. The zone experience is a natural condition. *Like sleep and sex, this profound and productive state is a mind/body process accessible to everyone.* In fact, if you are not consistently connecting with this high-performance experience, it is because you are *doing something* to block your natural response. Peak states are your inheritance. Flow is a natural process. You were born in the zone. My job is to help you find your way back.

IT Happens

CHAPTER | 2

Right now, imagine a lemon wedge. Now, imagine that you are popping that yellow, sour, juicy fruit slice into your mouth and biting down. Mouth watering? Congratulations, you have just passed Mind/Body Management 101. Using "information," you diverted the energy in your nervous system, changed the chemical makeup of your body, and turned on some very large organs. If you did not respond, find someone to take your pulse! This reaction is as natural as gravity. Since the invention of the tuba and trumpet, mischievous boys have been putting entire brass sections of marching bands out of operation by sucking lemons in view of the musicians.

How does the mental image of a lemon transform into a measurable physical reaction? Two words: *Information Transduction* (IT). Transduction simply means the conversion of energy from one form to another. Think of a waterwheel and the way water current is converted into electrical current. Moving water is transduced into mechanical energy by the turning of the wheel paddles, then further transduced, by a generator, into electrical energy, and, finally, transduced into light by an electric bulb.

Information Transduction refers to the same process when it takes place in your brain and body. While the exact mechanisms aren't known, something in the limbic-hypothalamic system of your brain takes the information contained in your thoughts and converts them into biological reactions that you experience and emotions that you feel.

You experience IT in action every day. Images of suspense up on the big screen transform into pounding hearts and feelings of excitement. Pizza commercials on the small one transduce into stomach contractions and craving. Thoughts of sex...well, you get the idea. But Information Transduction can do much more than just motivate you to dial out for Domino's or jumpstart your basic reactions. Tibetan monks use Information Transduction to stay alive during an extreme purification ritual in the Himalayas. At 14,000 feet, nearly naked and in temperatures approaching freezing, the monks meditate while wrapped in cold, wet sheets. The holy men not only beat hypothermia, they actually generate enough *real* physical heat to *dry* the icy sheets!

Transduction can also be deadly. In *five* separate incidents, the electrocardiograms of Air Force test pilots who had lost control of their aircraft and could not eject proved that the pilots were dead before they ever hit the ground. The pilots were killed by an idea, not by the actual event. The meditators and the unfortunate victims of "sudden death syndrome" are actually extreme ends of a broad continuum. The dividing line between the monks' biothermal marvel and the fighter pilots' deaths from fright comes down to information and how it was used. *The real "information highway" is the one that runs from your brain out to your body and back again.* While I am sure that you will continue to use the clothes dryer for your sheets, the dividing line between success and failure depends on how well you manage the transduction process. If IT can create dramatic flesh-and-blood changes, what can it do for your golf game, your sex life, or your energy level?

Michael Jordan is a master of Information Transduction. So are Jack Nicholson, Duke Ellington, and Mother Teresa. Exactly *how* did they transduce information into NBA championships, Academy Award performances, jazz, and unlimited compassion? They did the Transduction Two Step.

The Transduction Two Step

CHAPTER | 3

Mastering Information Transduction has fewer moves than the Hokey-Pokey. The personal-mastery dance simply requires that you *manage the information in your head and direct the energy in your body.* That's the Transduction Two Step and that's "what it's all about."

Information Management starts when you accept that *thoughts are things.* Like a drug or food, the type of information you take in, how much you take in, even when you take it in, makes a difference in how you feel and how you function. Now hear this: If you are not actively managing information, then information is managing you. When information is mismanaged or spins out of control, the mind locks up and the body acts out. You "know" that you are trying to sink the championship putt, but your body believes you are fighting for your life.

Energy Management starts with the basics of rest, good nutrition, and exercise, and ends when you can instantly create a relaxed and ready state even in the most challenging situations. Rest, nutrition, and exercise help you to master Information Transduction because it takes energy to run your body. Forty percent of your body is skeletal muscle, which can suck down energy at an enormous rate. Internal organs need energy to function. It is energy that flows along the neural pathways in the brain and out through the nervous system. Even emotions need energy to be generated. However, while these body basics can give you more power, real self-mastery comes from willfully directing the energy flow.

Starting today, you need to see mental and physical tension as the enemy. *Tension impedes performance and blocks your entry into the zone.* Look at your life and you can easily see how tension inhibits transduction's natural flow. Great sex, learning, and sleep are all inhibited by tension. Tight bodies have no follow-through on the golf course and can't "buy" a basket at the free throw line. Even memory and creativity are impeded by tension. Ever notice how difficult it is to remember a person's name during an introduction, but how easily the name pops into mind when it is no longer needed? Or how great ideas come to you in the shower or when you are driving the car, instead of the moments when you are trying to come up with something?

Watch what a child does when someone tells him or her to "Stop crying!" and you'll get a good idea of how most people manage their energy. To stop crying, the child tightens his throat, stomach, and back muscles, balls his hands into fists, and holds his breath. While this little display isn't exactly pretty, it does alter the energy flow physically and emotionally. Unfortunately, many people never learn any other way to respond to challenge. Thirty years later they are standing at the speaker's podium having the same reactions they had when they were in diapers, wondering "What's wrong with me?" In reality, the only thing that is wrong is the way they are using the First Rule. Water just doesn't flow easily through a kinked hose. Energy and information get bound up in a tight mind, rigid muscles, and overreacting organs.

It is time to turn information into something useful and to direct your energy supply. Information and Energy Management are *skills* you already know how to use. Peak living, higher performance, and physical power are only two steps away. Now put your left foot in…

> **When your only tool is a hammer,**
> **every problem becomes a nail.**
> —UNKNOWN—

A Word of Caution

CHAPTER | 4

The client in my office is a real comic. No, really, he does stand-up comedy. However, right now things aren't very funny. This comedian suffers from severe stage fright. He even performs a comedy routine about it, but he is not laughing at the moment. As we talk about Information and Energy Management, he becomes defensive and says, "You make it sound as if I'm doing these things to myself. I can't help it!" I tell him that, actually, I do think he is creating his fear and, if he wants to change, he best start thinking that way as well. The important truth is *what you create, you can control.*

Far too many of us hold the belief that our minds are working in opposition to our desires when, actually, your brain and body think they are doing you a favor. The sweaty palms on the first date, the shaking knees just before race time, and the dry mouth at the luncheon speech are all benefits. Your body is without direction and reacting the only way it knows how. When you choke on the tennis court, go blank during the final exam, or are inhibited on the dance floor, you feel like you "lost it" or you just don't "have it."

On the other hand, when you surprise yourself by making the clutch play, saying no to that seductive piece of cheesecake, or shining like a star in an important interview, you marvel, "I didn't know I had it in me." Sometimes you give "it" a name. You call "it" luck. Or you wonder how you can get "it" back again the next time you need "it." This is very confusing because *there is no "it."* You are not possessed. "It" isn't doing anything to you. The "it" you keep referring to is *your mind and body* and the way they have been *trained* to interact. In the absence of direction from you, "it" is making it up as it goes along. Succeeding or failing, *you are doing these things to yourself.*

My client doesn't have to get rid of his fear. He needs to take responsibility for generating it. To change the way he responds on stage, he must get off of "it" and start thinking in terms of "I." He must be able to answer two valuable questions: "What am I doing to myself?" and "How am I doing it?" As he learns to stop scaring himself, and starts managing information and energy, he will dramatically elevate the level of his performance. As he changes, "it" will seem to magically disappear. My client, the comic, can only begin to make this happen if he stops blaming "it" and starts to see his stage fright, with all its unpleasant physical sensations and uncomfortable emotions, as an opportunity. Accepting his situation as an opportunity to grow gives value to his suffering. Examining the system he uses to generate tension and fear shows him how he currently uses the First Mind Rule, and helps him discover what to do differently.

Here is the warning: Once you understand that it's IT not "it," you will lose the use of this universally accepted excuse. So read on only if you're ready to get "IT" on.

Where the Mind Goes, the Body and Emotions Follow

CHAPTER | 5

On May 10th, 1996, nine people lost their lives shortly after standing on the summit of the formidable Mount Everest. While the victims' deaths can be directly attributed to a rogue storm that ambushed the descending climbers, it was actually a succession of small mistakes and innocuous decisions that totaled up to catastrophe. The climbers on Mount Everest were killed by a series of cascading events. Crucial ropes weren't in place because of an argument between climbing teams. Strict rules about time and when to head back down the mountain were reduced to guidelines with fatal flexibility. One man's laser eye surgery failed at the high altitude, dividing the group. A lead member of the Sherpa team had exhausted himself the day before the climb, hauling around a heavy satellite phone for a wealthy climber. Standing alone, none of these errors would be life threatening. Cascading together, however, they led to one of the worst tragedies in climbing history.

Of course, as there are two sides to everything, the polar opposite of these negative cascading events are the positive occurrences that add up to life-altering incidents. You stop by to see a friend on a whim, and mention that you are on your way to a hockey game and have a spare ticket. Your friend has a cold and can't go but his cousin from Alaska, who happens to be in town because her flight was canceled, is a big hockey fan and would be happy to join you. You go with the cousin to the game, have a great time, get married, and raise six children.

Life is a series of cascading events, and Information Transduction is a cascading event that takes place inside of you. The First Rule is like a weathervane that points to these events as they unfold within your brain and your body and become your life experience or level of performance. Just as a weathervane tracks the wind, the First Rule points the direction that Information Transduction is headed. Instead of the cardinal points of north, east, west, and south, the First Rule tracks information and energy as they move through the four markers of human health and growth—the mental, physical, emotional, and behavioral sides of your life. In essence, the First Rule slows down the transduction process so that you can observe it in action and alter its course.

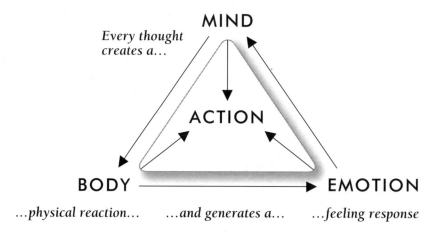

THE TRANSDUCTION TRIANGLE

"Where the mind goes, the body and emotions follow," is a simple little epigram that calls attention to an important fact: *Each thought you have creates a physical reaction in your body and generates the emotions that you feel.* Seen through the eyes of the First Rule, life becomes a revolving door of ideas affecting the body, the body generating emotional reactions, and these feelings, in turn, driving behavior and influencing thinking. The good news is that each phase of the transduction process is an opportunity to transform, interfere with, or enhance information and energy as they are converted into action. Now it is time to get personal.

About twenty-five hundred years ago, a very wise man, Siddhartha Gautama, said that personal growth comes when you "Take responsibility for your own development and directly investigate the nature of your experience." As we explore the First Rule, investigate your experience and see if you can detect how IT is affecting your life and your performance. Don't just focus on the negative. Search for the patterns that put you in, or at least near, the zone. Observation leads to insight. Insight is information. Information becomes physical energy and emotion. All three culminate in action. You see, the more accurate information you have about the way you currently use the First Rule, the faster you'll move into a more powerful and productive cycle.

Take IT from the Top

CHAPTER | 6

According to a bold, new theory, information happened on the scene seconds after the Big Bang and immediately took a job as the organizational principle of the universe. Apparently, what started as cycles of resonance in the primal soup of the cosmos grew increasingly complex, until it *evolved* into biological systems and *became* the highly advanced system of information called mankind. Today, psychology, biology, and physics recognize information as the crucial, connecting link between all the arts and sciences. From the molecules and the genes in every living cell, to international corporations, governments, and the developing patterns of your interpersonal relationships, *all systems use information to form and to function.* As a highly advanced informational system, you use words, images, and perceptions to process information.

The First Rule fires up when incoming information and input from the five senses (sight, touch, taste, hearing, smell) mingle with stored knowledge and impressions from the four basic perceptions (light, time, temperature, and awareness of your body's position, weight, and movement). Switching into self-organizing mode, your brain draws in related ideas and begins linking them into a series or a chain of thoughts. Like the tiny atom, each thought contains tremendous potential power but, at this stage, information is still unorganized and unstable. The slightest distraction or smallest addition or subtraction of a fact or detail can quickly derail the transduction process.

Like atomic fusion, thoughts must bond together to form concepts before they can initiate the chain reaction that eventually becomes the explosion of our actions. Heart transplants, moon exploration, and even the horror of the Holocaust all began as random or idle thoughts that coalesced into concepts and became movements. However, before concepts reach critical mass they need a catalyst. When it comes to Information Transduction, that catalyst is your Imagination.

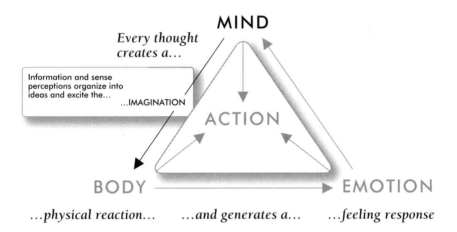

Imagination Is Everything

When baseball legend Hank Aaron was asked how he hit so many home runs he answered, "I slow the ball down and make it bigger." Obviously Aaron didn't actually alter the physical size or speed of the ball. Those hardballs came at him with the same 90 to 100 mph velocity as toward everyone else. Hank Aaron coordinated his timing, prepared his muscles, and manipulated his perception through the skillful use of his mind's greatest resource, the "creative intelligence."

Musical scores, self-talk, boy noises like cheering crowds and squealing tires, imagery, and symbols of power are just some of the pathways that information travels as it transforms into energy. As information and imagination fuse, ideas explode into life and onto the scene. No longer idle, these fully animated ideas move out from the confines of your brain, travel along your extended nervous system, and engage your body. *Your imagination is the creative link connecting mind and body.*

Think back to your experience with the lemon. To kick the saliva glands into action, all you had to do was imagine a lemon; mind/body momentum took over from there. Your creative intelligence is the force that drives the First Rule to the next level. The English language is loaded with colloquial references to this explosion in the thinking process. We say that imagination "runs away with you," "blows your mind," and "plays tricks." Even today we try to shut down the imagination before we get "carried away" and "go there." It seems that the same force that gives life to the "monster under the bed" holds the power to put you in the zone.

The tools of internal creativity give you direct access to the First Rule, and managing them well usually spells the difference between being the hero and just being afraid. To develop sheet-drying body heat, the Tibetan monks imagined a "fire or heat that comes from the universe" and travels through a "central vessel of the body." Hank Aaron perceived a fastball in slow motion to beat the Babe's home run record. Basketball players win championships by "hearing" a swoosh and "seeing" a super-sized hoop before they shoot. The shadow in the dark alley or the unexpected late-night phone call needs a little creativity in order to become a panic attack. The symbols, images, and self-talk may change, but the tool remains the same. Imagination makes thinking *real* by *activating* the body. Your ability to use the First Mind Rule depends on making imagination your ally.

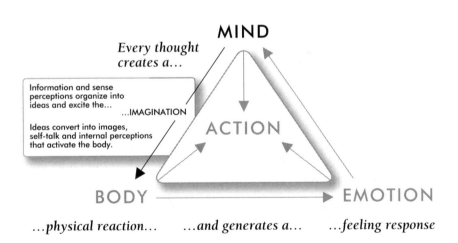

Every thought creates a...

Information and sense perceptions organize into ideas and excite the...
...IMAGINATION

Ideas convert into images, self-talk and internal perceptions that activate the body.

MIND

ACTION

BODY ⟶ EMOTION

...physical reaction...   ...and generates a...   ...feeling response

Let's Get Physical

CHAPTER | 8

In the year 840, Emperor Leo of Bavaria died when he saw a solar eclipse for the first, and obviously last, time. The Emperor expired when his imagination and body collided. Like the unfortunate test pilots who passed on before their disabled aircraft crashed into the ground, Emperor Leo's body was overloaded by the rapid influx of energy as it transduced down from creatively enhanced information. Unlike the unlucky pilots, however, Leo was never in any real danger; a solar eclipse isn't life threatening, but then neither is a job interview, the clutch-play in the tournament, being a single parent, or taking an important test. Speaking in public might not be deadly, but for the majority of Americans it feels that way!

When your information management skills are low and your imagination is overactive, your body quickly loads up with energy. Muscles tense, adrenals pump, and the immune system is compromised. As your brain and body try to compensate for this overload, they dump energy, which can leave you feeling weak and drained just when you need strength and power the most. Your body has taken creative direction from your mind and now it takes control. Information Transduction is having its way with you just as it did with poor Emperor Leo. At this point, all the "positive thinking" in the world won't stop this mind/body merry-go-round, and it would take the informational equivalent of electroshock therapy to get you back under control. *Once information "gets physical," you're going to have to deal directly with energy and let that action be positive feedback for the mind.*

Direct intervention with the physical forces inside of you is nothing new. Anytime you tried to counteract the effects of energy overload by counting to ten, taking a deep breath, or sighing out loud, you were on the right track. These simple strategies are actually very effective. However, to respond to challenge with power, grace, and precision, you must go a step farther and open up the lines of communication between your conscious intent and the power in your body that makes things happen.

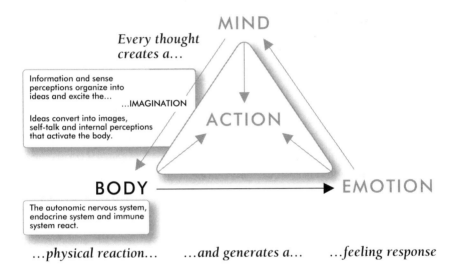

Energy Management means that you can *control your rate of transduction and direct your nervous system*. For now, it is just important to see that the First Rule is a force that affects you physically and emotionally. As thoughts cascade from intangible "mind stuff" into flesh-and-blood realities, emotions are born.

Feeling Energy

CHAPTER | 9

Oscar-winning performances happen when actors get into character and convince us that they really are dying, deeply in love, or on the edge of a breakdown. Surrounded by bright lights, a film crew, and a camera lens about the size of Ohio, these actors are able to reach inside of themselves and *create* the powerful emotions that they project into the characters they play.

Many actors find their motivation through a process developed by Konstantin Stanislavsky known as "method acting." Not surprisingly, the "method" mirrors the First Rule. Focusing attention on a *concept*, like a past memory or an imagined fantasy, these actors then *remove tension from their bodies* and allow the emerging emotions to take over. While *no one directly controls their feelings,* method actors use their minds and bodies to bring up the emotions they need, when they need them. This is a handy trick if you want to build motivation, maintain grace under fire, or grow during life's difficult times.

If you have ever cut out a quote or saying from a newspaper or magazine and posted it on your refrigerator, or carried it around in your wallet, then you are already tinkering with the emotional side of the First Rule. Inspiring stories, like all important information, are *processed* by your body and transformed into comfort or strength. In fact, important ideas actually *need* to be "emotionalized." Success seems hollow until you internalize your achievements. Closure never comes if you think grief is a four-letter-word. Life seems flat unless you occasionally feel some joy. More importantly, as the energy of the body is converted into emotion, you are propelled forward into *action.*

Like it or not, it is *your emotions that drive your actions;* you spend your life doing what you *feel* like doing. We all do. Guilt keeps us honest. Confidence allows us to take risks. You give up on the diet because you *feel* like eating pizza. Paying taxes is a byproduct of not wanting to step into the ring with the IRS. In our society, "I did" or "I didn't" is joined at the hip with "I feel" or "I felt." Right or wrong, action follows feelings. Managing emotional energy gives you the discipline not to be swayed by whims, indulgences, or moods. Instead you learn to amplify your natural passion and power and leap into the zone.

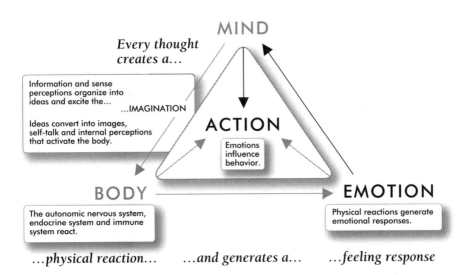

The Next Wave

CHAPTER | 10

The difference between dreaming and doing is in how you use the First Rule. How you handle information and energy, as it transduces down the line, ultimately determines your conduct and the quality of your performance. If you *conceptualize* exercise as a painful affair that is doomed to fail while you *imagine* yourself as an immense blob of fat stuffed into a spandex leotard flailing your way through some aerobics class, you are not likely to *feel* like rushing down to the gym. If the next wave of transduction involves information about how tired you are, while you imagine yourself stretched out on the couch bathed in the warm light of the TV and feeling comfy, you aren't going anywhere. Like the challenger in a prizefight who sees himself as the overmatched underdog, you are defeated before the first blow is thrown.

When information has gotten out of hand, you move to the second stage of the Transduction Two Step and manage your energy by managing your actions. If transduction has gone beyond the thinking, imagining, and feeling stage, you still have the power to influence the process. *In the long run, no matter what you think, imagine, or feel, it is what you do that matters.* As the First Rule unfolds into action, transduction *is altered by your behavior.*

Everyone who has pushed through inertia, put on their running shoes, and "did it" anyway, knows the feeling of euphoria and pride that follows. The boxer who steps into the ring, despite his fear, is already a champion whatever the outcome of the fight. *The more control you have over your actions, the greater the influence you have on the next wave of transduction.* Once emotion transforms into action,

action transforms back into information. The feedback you get from what you do and how you do it alters the information that you process in your body and that you experience as emotion. This is how saying "no" to a piece of cheesecake or an alcoholic beverage and sticking with your eating plan or sobriety directly translates into elevated feelings of self-esteem and confidence.

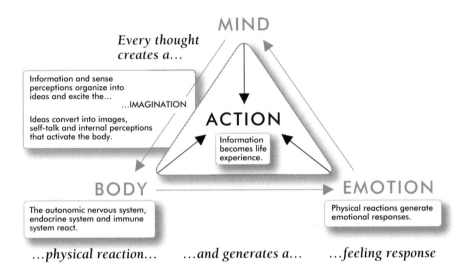

...physical reaction...   *...and generates a...*   *...feeling response*

In theory, information that moves through the transduction process should produce wisdom. Unfortunately, feedback can be used to reinforce old attitudes. Either way, *you become what you transduce.* Why? Positive or negative, all the information cycling through the transduction process establishes a pathway from the brain out to the body and back again. Important information is given a priority line and *enhanced* to transduce more rapidly. This makes the process more automatic, which is great if you are transducing an awesome backhand; but it also makes it less accessible, which is bad if you are struggling with fear or gripped by regret. For better or worse, information endowed with "enhanced transduction" is *allowed unlimited access to power.*

The IT Test

CHAPTER | **11**

PRETEST INSTRUCTIONS

This is a test. For the next five minutes we will be conducting a test of your Information Transduction skills. Hidden in this simple process are all the elements necessary for transducing ideas and images into the perfect golf shot, the energy to fight depression, or the creative discipline to write an award-winning bestseller. The test should shed some light on your current ability to *intentionally* utilize the Information Transduction system.

You will *not* be able to think your way to a passing grade. In fact, the more you try to apply logic and reason to the IT Test, the more difficult it will become. What seems a little strange or silly at first, is actually a rare glimpse of a profound process going on just below the surface, every moment of every day. Don't *try* to make anything happen. You have far more intimate experience with this process than you might imagine; just follow the simple instructions.

THE TEST

Begin by standing or sitting up, straight. Extend both your arms directly out in front of you with the palms of your hands facing each other. Keep your palms 6 to 8 inches apart. Take in a breath and relax your shoulders.

Concentrate on the empty space between your hands and start to think about magnets. Magnets you have held. Cartoon magnets you have seen. Imagine any and all kinds of magnets and think about that magnetic energy between your hands, pulling them together. Imagine that you have a pair of magnets strapped to each palm or that you are wearing magnetic gloves or that your hands *are* magnets. Now think about those magnets pulling and tugging your hands closer and closer together. Close your eyes, concentrate and imagine the *feeling* of the magnets pulling your hands closer and closer together. Now just concentrate on the pulling and pulsing of the magnets. Do this for 2 minutes or until your two hands touch.

OR

Start by standing or sitting up tall in a chair. Take a full breath in and relax your neck and shoulders as you exhale. Press your palms together and begin to rub them vigorously. As you do, imagine that energy is building up in your hands.

After about 30 seconds, stop and extend you arms out in front of you. Keep the palms facing each other, about 6 to 8 inches apart. Now imagine a force or an energy pulsing or flowing between your two hands, pulling them together or pushing them apart. Close your eyes at the end of this sentence and imagine a powerful force moving between your hands for a minute or two.

SCORING

Your response is the barometer for testing your skill. Like the ultimate biofeedback machine, your response measures your ability to consciously convert information into action. You responded well if you could quickly *feel* the magnets or the pulsing force. You responded better if you found that you could both feel the force *and* control its intensity or change its direction. You responded best if you felt the energy, took control in some way, *and* found that the process helped you to concentrate or left you physically energized. You did not respond so well if you found yourself stuck analyzing the process, with tired arms and feelings of frustration.

Obviously an easier, stronger, and longer response is desired, but don't be discouraged if you have less than a powerful experience at first. The nonlinear nature of the mind/body response wreaks havoc with your ingrained thinking processes. Managing transduction requires you to route energy from your brain into your muscles and nerves and back again, unimpeded. Critical thinking creates cortical constipation and cuts you off from your natural response. Energy that could be flowing down into the body is getting locked up, literally at the top of your head. The instant you stop analyzing the process and begin to focus on the "magnets," you start to manage information and direct energy.

A GOOD QUESTION

Are we dealing with "real" energy here? That is a very good question, one which I cannot answer. Western science says that this force does not exist because it cannot be measured, but Oriental medicine counters that human beings *are* the only instruments sensitive enough to detect this type of power. You choose. But active force or imagined sensation, the energy does *feel* real, and for our purposes, it is the "feel of IT" that is important. For now, delete the need to judge and simply observe your response. Get the energy flowing into the body by relaxing your neck and shoulders and stay focused on the feeling of the pulling and pushing of the magnetic force.

If you are having trouble, take heart; in hundreds of seminars, I have watched lawyers, accountants, and engineers, all individuals with a well-developed bias for critical thinking, learn to jump neurological pathways and bypass this energy blockage in the brain. If you are still having difficulty, take the IT Test at night when your critical thinking process is too tired to interfere, or first thing in the morning before it has a chance to fully organize. Whatever your response, keep playing with this process! The key to peak living and higher performance is hidden within this little puzzle.

The Structure of Transduction

CHAPTER | 12

Albert Einstein struggled with algebra. In fact, he was failing the subject until a concerned uncle intervened. How did Einstein's uncle get him out of academic trouble and on his way to the Theory of Relativity? He helped young Albert to tune up his transduction. But before I tell you exactly what he did, let's return to the "waterwheel example" of Information Transduction.

Moving water becomes mechanical energy through the turning of the paddle wheel. Mechanical energy is then transduced, by a generator, into electrical energy, and is then further transduced into light by an electric bulb. Along the way, this process is made possible by the shafts, gears, electrical coils and wires, filaments in the light bulb, and even the nuts, bolts, and wood that form the structure of the waterwheel. If you wanted to repair the waterwheel or improve its capacity to generate power, these are the parts that you would have to change, upgrade, or lubricate.

The same is true for Information and Energy Management. Your thoughts are the moving water; your imagination is the turning blades. Your body is the mechanical gears and shafts; your emotion is the generator that powers the light bulb of your actions. Just as hydrogen and oxygen are the basic components of water, *words and attention* are two of the major elements that create thinking. *Self-talk and imagery* are paddles on the wheel of the imagination. *Muscle tension, breathing, rest, and nutrition* are a few of the nuts and bolts that directly affect your physical and emotional structure. *Behavior* is the foundation on which everything sits. It is time to pull out your internal toolbox and give yourself a mind-body tune-up. In Part II you will learn exactly what adjustments control the Mind's First Rule and how to work with Information Transduction.

How did Einstein's uncle transform failure into a lifelong love affair with physics? The answer lies in simple Information Management. Albert's uncle asked his nephew three questions. Did young Albert like math? The reply was a sullen, "No." Did he like playing cops and robbers? The reply was an enthusiastic, "Yes!" Then asked the uncle, "Why don't you pretend that the 'X' in your algebra equation is a fugitive and you are the detective trying to find him?" Young Albert's concepts were transformed, his imagination was ignited, his body and emotions became energized, and the action it produced transformed all our lives, forever. Now *that* is IT!

Information Management

Mind Games

CHAPTER | 13

In a classic Zen story, two monks are arguing about a temple flag that is waving in the breeze. The first monk said that the flag moved, the second countered that it was actually the wind that moved. The master of the monastery quickly ended the debate by saying, "It is neither the flag nor the wind, but your mind that moves."

"Reality" is a word that demands quotation marks. And in today's era of "spin," reality has become very flexible indeed. While one cable news program is yelling, "The flag is responsible," the next one will be screaming, "It's the wind, stupid!" Both programs will have research and experts to back up their claims. Both will stand by their version of the "truth." In the early morning hours, each channel will feature an author who believes that the flag is a hoax and that the wind is part of a vast conspiracy.

If you are honest about it, outside of undeniable laws like gravity or the fact that it is raining, "reality" is almost always a choice. In the stock market crash of 1929, the businessmen who focused on catastrophe and failure jumped to their deaths from the newly built Empire State Building. The people in the office next door, who chose to focus on damage control and forward thinking, lived to prosper in the recovery that came less than a decade later. In the end, how you choose to use your *attention*, the way in which you choose to engage your *imagination*, and the manner in which you choose to *communicate* will shape your reality.

Attention, imagination, and communication are the three tools of Information Management. Focusing your attention on how you shirt clings to you in the humidity, while imagining the thermometer's red tip rising and chanting variations of "I'm so hot," "It's so hot," and "This IS THE hottest," won't actually elevate the outside temperature but it will increase your discomfort, and that *is* your reality. Paying attention to a faint breeze, imagining the body's natural cooling process of evaporation taking place, and talking about almost anything *but* the heat and how awful you feel won't change the fact that it's 105 degrees, but you *will* cope more effectively. Think that's a bunch of horse hooey? Athletes who race in the Hawaiian Ironman Triathlon face intense heat, as well as wind and fatigue, while biking and running along the scorching Kona coast. Skillfully utilizing attention, imagination, and communication, these athletes not only elevate their body's comfort level, they train their nervous system to thrive in the heat.

The difference between realizing dreams and outright failure, and the dividing line between peak performance and flailing effort, is determined in the moments just before the nervous system comes on line and the emotions begin to flow, the time when attention, imagination, and communication *rule* transduction. Legendary mental discipline and masterful execution belong to those who can skillfully wield the three tools of Information Management.

ATTENTION

The Tale of Two Wolves

CHAPTER | 14

The young chief went to see the elder medicine man and told him, "A terrible fight is going on inside me and it is between two wolves. One is the wolf of arrogance, anger, and greed. The other is the wolf of compassion, peace, and benevolence. Can you tell me which wolf will win?" "Yes," replied the holy man, "The wolf who wins will be the one that you feed."

Just what *does* wildlife on the internal frontier eat? *Attention.* Brain research suggests that you have approximately 60,000 thoughts throughout the course of a single day. Unfortunately, the same research also indicates that nearly 90 percent of those 60,000 thoughts are the exact thoughts that you had yesterday, and the day before that, and the day before that. In other words, a tremendous amount of attention is centered on a relatively small nucleus of ideas. These dense concentrations of thought generally have a theme that can be classified under one of two broad headings. The first wolf might be called "life-affirming" because it is the wolf of possibility. These are the thoughts, emotions, and behaviors that are proactive, encourage creativity, and promote life. The second wolf is "life-negating." This wolf is made up of the concepts, sensations, and actions that work against growth, restrict flow, or terminate life.

This life-negating wolf does have its place. Weeds in the garden need pulling. War must sometimes be waged. Skepticism can be healthy when dealing with people who have their own interests foremost in mind. But feed the wolf of pessimism the lion's share of your thoughts, and all you will transduce is chronic stress, fear, and stilted performance. The struggling salesperson who focuses on bad news about the economy or his company is no different than the rock climber whose attention is consumed with ideas and images of falling, pain, and death. Too much attention to the problem creates mental and physical paralysis and overloads the body with emotional energy. The only way out of the dead-end alley of negative focus is in *redirecting attention* to where you want it to go. Patients with cancer or heart problems must face the life-negating wolf that comes in the form of their diagnosis, but they must switch their attention to the life-affirming wolf when it comes to the prognosis. And the battle cry of the life-affirming wolf is, "I can!"

A Carnegie-Mellon/University of Miami study showed that the coronary bypass surgery patients who recovered the quickest, with the least complications, were the patients who approached their recovery in a "directed, goal-orientated way." These patients *participated* in their recovery as opposed to merely *observing* the process. They sought information on what they could do to help themselves heal, took action, and even made plans for when they would be released from the hospital.

Like the salesman, the rock climber, and the cancer patient, you must acknowledge the wolf of the worst-case scenario so that you can assess the real gravity and consequences of your situation, but to *transduce power you must quickly shift your attention to what you want, your strategy for getting it, and the resources at your disposal.* To overcome adversity or to elevate your game, you must seek out and feed the wolf of opportunity. Start by directing your attention to your assets, choices, and support systems. Read the biographies of the courageous and study the stories of their success.

The evening of September 11th 2001, I had had enough of the television coverage of the terrorist attack and the aftermath of the tragedy. All day my focus of attention was exactly where it should have been: assessing the threat to myself, my family, and my country.

I turned off CNN and took my attention out to my office. With the desk lamp turned down low, I sat in the half light and listened to the most poignant and rousing speeches I could find on the Internet, talks that were given by great men in times of peril and uncertainty. Through the voices, words, and wisdom of Churchill, Kennedy, and Roosevelt, I transduced perspective, courage, and power. Others had been here. We would rise to the challenge. We would prevail.

In the confusing days that followed, I kept my eye on the conflict that dominated the headlines, but I also looked to history, to that "torch of freedom" that had now been passed to "a new generation of Americans," and in that information I found strength, clarity, and meaning.

Which wolf will you feed today?

The Information Diet

CHAPTER | 15

In the next 24 hours, you will take in as much information as a person during the medieval age absorbed in an entire lifetime. The 10 P.M. news, e-mail, a coworker's constant complaining, information about a family conflict, news of an upcoming promotion, or questions about buying a new car will need to be transduced. Work details, traffic, phone numbers, headlines, TV, advertising, elevator music, and even gossip will be converted into physical reactions and have emotional repercussions. It is as if information has us all under attack. Worse, research suggests that your brain craves new information the way your taste buds desire chocolate or a cold beer!

The novelty-seeking part of the brain, also known as the Ascending Reticular Activating System (ARAS), is a complex information processor that runs from the organ's basic memory and pain-pleasure centers all the way up to the higher cortical areas and thinking functions. Ever wonder how a new mother can sleep through the regular nightly noises but be awake instantly if her baby even whimpers? Thank the novelty-seeking part of the brain. Live near an airport or busy freeway and find that, over time, you get used to the noise. Again, it's the brain's automatic information manager hard at work. Unfortunately, the ARAS is a sucker for anything sparkly and unique and is designed to endlessly "channel surf" through your life experience. Important goals and dreams and invaluable lessons become dated bits of discarded information that are shoved into the background by the exciting news that this year's "it" girl has just been discovered. Your ARAS needs a diet, an *Information Diet.*

The Information Diet, like its physical counterpart, doesn't mean that you stop taking in information. That is as impossible as living without eating. You need information in order to function. As with any successful eating plan, your Information Diet works best as a long-term lifestyle change rather than a drastic attempt to trim down in time for bikini season. Read instead of watching TV. Treat mindless media or blown-out-of-proportion news reporting as if it were junk food for your brain; it is fun once in a while but not healthy as a steady diet. Make it a point to avoid gossip and stop wasting energy transducing grist from the rumor mill. Intensify your listening and responding skills so that you process much of the information *in the conversation* and not afterward. Spend some time transducing quiet.

Lastly, avoid ingesting large quantities of information before bedtime. Sixty million Americans suffer from frequent or chronic sleep problems. For many of these people, insomnia is actually a case of *information indigestion*. They take in too much information, too late in the day, and then process it all night long. Gorging on information before going to sleep will do more than give you bad dreams, it will shape the way you think and feel about life.

Remember, it is the job of the ARAS to designate which information will be transduced into a *heightened biological state*. So give your goals and dreams the attention they need by "spicing" them with ideas that are both new and novel. Review the latest research in your chosen field. Investigate, explore, and compile stories about people you want to emulate and the approach they use to achieve success. Feed your mind quality information about who you want to be, where you want to go, when you want to be there, and transduction will make it so.

Within You, Without You

CHAPTER | 16

Sometime in the early 1920's, Dr. Carl Jung discovered that attention is like a bellybutton; some people are "inneys" while others are "outies." Jung noticed that some people preferred to focus their attention on the external environment around them, while others tended to concentrate their attention more toward the world inside themselves. Even his fellow psychiatrists and their theories fit the pattern. Sigmund Freud, with his focus of attention on the external desire for pleasure as mankind's driving force, was an outie. Albert Alder, who focused on man's need to compensate for his internal inferiority complex, was an inney.

Jung missed his chance to use this bellybutton analogy and, instead, called the tendency to look out to the world "extroversion" (from the Latin "extra"—outside) and the inward focus "introversion" (from the Latin "intro"—inside). As these words found their way into common use, they became stereotypes. Inneys were thought to be ninnies because they were shy, self-conscious, and socially awkward. Outies were looked on as rowdies because they were always doing something *out*rageous in a desperate attempt to be recognized. Popular thinking perverted Dr. Jung's beautiful theory of orientation into two unrecognizable dictums: If you contemplated your own bellybutton you were self-absorbed; if you wanted others to contemplate your bellybutton you were shallow.

In truth, being an inney or outie just means that you have a *natural preference* for how you use your attention and process information. Introverts process information internally, which takes time and often makes them look awkward or seem aloof. Extroverts do their information processing on the fly and in public, which accounts for their outreaching and sometimes brash behavior. While your preference for focusing your attention is as defined and ingrained as being right- or left-handed, Dr. Jung felt that there was a great deal to be learned from understanding and utilizing your nondominant side.

Inneys can waste a lifetime wandering in their internal universe, disconnected from the magnificent experience going on all around them. Outies can search forever outside of themselves for strength, happiness, or truth only to find out, in the end, that the answers were always waiting inside. Since you must be present to win the prize in the raffle of life, extending your attention outward allows you to be and do your best right here, right now. On the flip side, inward attention gives clarity to life's purpose and position while connecting you to the profound resources that wait in your deeper nature.

Your preference for inward or outward focus maybe as fixed as the position of your navel, but understanding how to work with both sides of your attention quickly translates to external power and inner discipline.

E.S.P.

CHAPTER | 17

What do a pair of golf shoes, the color of the car parked next to yours, and the song of a bird have in common? They are all opportunities to sharpen your E.S.P. Not the *Extra* Sensory Perception that foretells the future, but rather *Enhanced* Sensory Perception, which may not help you to pick this week's winning lottery numbers but which will immediately improve your performance and dramatically increase the quality of your life.

All that is required is that you focus your attention *out* through the windows of your five senses and onto your here-and-now experience. Focusing your attention on the feel of your golf cleats as they sink into the green, the awareness of the details and objects in your environment, or the simple act of closely listening, will pull you into the present and intensify your power. And, according to Dr. Ruth herself, techniques like Enhanced Sensory Perception will also improve your sex life!

To sharpen your outward focus of attention, chose a sensory experience (taste, hearing, sight, smell, touch) and focus your full attention on that experience. When you are eating, experience tasting. When you become aware of a sound, listen with full attention and experience the process called hearing. Look at what you are looking at; study it with your eyes. Sounds simple enough, right? There is a catch or two.

Catch one comes when you find that your mind doesn't "mind" very well, and it seems determined to turn your attention inward. One minute you are focused on the feel of the leather wrapped around the club handle and the next, you are *planning* your calendar, *imagining* an upcoming conversation, or *remembering* a past event. Planning, imagining, or remembering are road signs indicating that your attention has turned around and headed back inside.

Catch two is the relentlessly judgmental nature of the mind. Critical assessment and emotional judgment have their place, but assessing the pros and cons and likes or dislikes of your sensory experience draws your attention inward and away from your purpose. To keep your attention on the outside, you must *delete the need to analyze or judge* and focus your mind on the information coming in from your senses.

What can you expect from tackling and directing your attention to the world outside? Focusing outward and observing without judgment shortens your reaction time while increasing power and fluid movement. Focusing outward gives you a break from your internal images of worry and fear and allows the unconscious part of the creative process to take a crack at finding a solution to the problem. Focusing outward makes life fun.

To know and to act are one and the same.

—SAMURAI MAXIM—

The E.S.P. Exercise

CHAPTER | 18

While it is probably best to practice this exercise out in nature, don't wait for your next camping trip to get started. Dedicate a specific span of time from one minute to one hour and concentrate your attention on your sensory experience. Look at your immediate surroundings and focus your attention on that experience. Look out into the distance and notice what is there. Repeat the word "seeing" as you visually take in the object or environment. The critical mind is like a five-year-old who stays out of trouble when given something to do. Silently repeating "seeing" gives judgment a task and helps key in concentration. Soon these words actually become sensory cues that *create* outward focus, but more on that later. For now, just stay with the experience of seeing for a few seconds or a few minutes and then shift your attention to hearing.

Listen intently to the sounds around you and silently repeat the word "hearing." Notice the sounds close to you. Listen to the ones in the far-off distance. Then move on to "touching." Notice the pressure, texture, temperature, and weight of anything in your hands, clothes against skin, or the cushions of a chair against your body.

When you find yourself wandering inward (and you will), *note what you are doing*—are you planning, remembering, or just lost in a fantasy? Then, take your attention and turn it back outward. Just repeat the key word and zero back in on your experience. Part of the power of this process comes from catching your attention as it swings inward and directing your focus back outward.

Keep moving and rotate through all the five senses, including taste and smell. After you have moved through all five senses, let them merge together. You're done. Linger on any sense you would like for as long as you like or rotate through the process several times.

In the E.S.P. exercise, there are no real rules beyond staying externally focused and suspending judgment. The exercise costs nothing and can be practiced anywhere because you take your senses with you wherever go. Standing in line at the grocery store is as good a place to practice as the quiet comfort of your home. You can keep your eyes open, and no one needs to know what you are doing. Soon you'll be using the outward focus exercises for those times when it is important for you to be present. From stepping up to the proverbial plate when you're needed the most, to spending intimate time with someone you love, Enhanced Sensory Perception becomes a segue to performing and living at your peak.

> *Life is not a problem to be solved*
> *but a reality to be experienced.*
> —KIERKEGAARD—

More Fun with Outward Focus

CHAPTER | 19

Spending most of his life in exile from his home in Tibet, the Dalai Lama has seen his share of motel rooms. Asked by a reporter in Santa Barbara, California, what the first thing was that he did when he came into a new room, the Dalai Lama replied, "I look for something unique or interesting about this particular place."

Since your mind is *automatically* seeking the new and novel anyway, why not put it to use and pull yourself into the present at the same time? Make a mental note at the start of your day to *seek* out something unique in your immediate environment. Search for something in your everyday world that you have never seen before. Be on the lookout for the color red as you go through your day. Listen for laughter and the sounds of wildlife. Look for something unique in the architecture or landscape near where you live. Note the shape and color of the eyes of each person that you speak with today.

As time goes by, get more specific about your search. Look for people wearing white hats or shoes, or listen for words, mottoes, or names you have never heard before. Each time you encounter the designated item, let it act as a mental cue to turn your attention outward. Set your mind searching for the novel, and you will spend more time focused in the now.

The Looking Glass of Attention

CHAPTER | 20

When Alice stepped through the looking glass, she entered a strange world where she had very little control. When it comes to harnessing inward attention, a lot of people feel like Alice. Comfortable or not, exercises like those presented here are the gateway to mental discipline. Not only are they the antidote to information overload and a means for becoming centered and solid when facing a challenge, they are a key component in the mind-body learning process.

Luckily, the process of focusing inward is actually quite simple. It only requires that you close your eyes, create a visual image, and hold that image in your mind for two minutes. Any single image, like the static image of a landscape or the number 6 written on a blackboard, is fine. You could also imagine a series of sequential events that are unfolding, such as a candle burning, a bird flying, or a stream of running water. For now, stay with simple images that are free of emotional content. Focusing inward on the face of someone you love or imagining a pleasant memory will generate warm feelings, but that is not the purpose of this exercise. Let's build a strong base before we move on.

1) Choose an image: a glass of milk/a red triangle/ a series of numbers/a candle flame.

2) Focus on the image as clearly as possible. While not everyone "sees" the equivalent of an internal television set, everyone can imagine. Even the person who can't visualize a glass of milk *can* tell you whether it is hot

or cold by the steam coming off the top or
the droplets of condensation running down
the side. Sometimes, imagining the images as
if on TV, projected onto a blank movie screen,
or written out on a blackboard gives you
something to hang your visualization hat on.
Just bring the image up, make it as clear as
you can, and stay with it.

3) Hold the image in your mind for two minutes.
One hundred twenty seconds is a long time
to the undisciplined mind. Most likely your
mind will wander. Just notice when it does
and gently bring your mind back to the image.
Remember, some difficulty at the beginning
is to be expected. Even if it seems that all you
are doing is catching your mind as it wanders
off and bringing it back, you are building the
muscles that control attention.

How to use the exercise: Several times during the day when it is
appropriate and safe to do so, pick an image, close your eyes, focus
on the image, and hold it in your mind's eye for two minutes.

What you can expect: As you become proficient at directing your
attention inward, this exercise will produce a centering effect.
Centering isn't just some airy, New Age term. When you focus your
mind on these *neutral*, internal images, you change the way you use
your brain and literally bring the two major branches of the
autonomic nervous system into balance. You are creating greater
equilibrium in your body, causing you to feel centered. Over time,
you will find that your ability to stay focused and concentrate will
improve, and you will be able to hold the image for longer
periods with greater clarity.

The Concentration Game

CHAPTER | 21

If attention were a muscle, the Concentration Game would be the bench press of mental workouts. Integrated as part of almost every system of martial arts, the Concentration Game helps you quickly gain access to your attention and give direction to your focus. During this exercise, you will be building your attention muscles by attending to the simple experience of breathing. Once again, your mind will attempt to hook you into one of its three favorite functions: planning, remembering, or thinking. Refuse to take the bait. Rather, note that your mind has wandered and go back to the experience of breathing. If you are feeling frustrated because your mind wanders off so easily, note that as well and redirect your attention back to your breathing.

As you play, do not force the air in or out of your lungs; just breathe naturally. Pay close attention to your chest as it raises and lowers. Focus on the physical experience of the lungs expanding and deflating or the sensation of air as it moves past the openings in your nose. Let's play a round of the Concentration Game:

Sit down, either in chair or on a cushion on the floor. Close your eyes and get comfortable. If you choose to recline or lay down, keep your arms and legs uncrossed. Become aware of your breathing. Let it become slow, deep, and natural. Take in a full breath and think the number "1" silently to yourself. Count the breath and keep your mind focused on the feeling of breathing. Notice how your chest, back, and abdominal muscles expand out as you inhale. Feel your lungs as they inflate. Then exhale slowly and gently. As you become aware of the muscles letting go and the air leaving your lungs, count "2." Again, let go of all thoughts except the thought of "2" and your experience of breathing. On the next inhalation count "3," and when you exhale think "4." Continue this process all the way up to "10." Then begin again at "1."

Stay focused on the number and the sensation of breathing. Whenever you are distracted by a thought, a feeling, or a physical sensation, and you lose track of where you are, just make a mental note of it and begin again at "1." The numbers in themselves are unimportant; they are simply a device to help you train your attention.

How to use the exercise: Like the three previous exercises, you can work the Concentration Game into your daily activities. Simply grab two minutes in your day and when it is safe and appropriate to do so, close your eyes and focus your attention on your breathing process, counting the breaths from "1" to "10."

An even better way to practice this exercise is to carve out some time during your day, go to a place where you will not be disturbed, and practice the Concentration Game for an extended period. Start with a five-minute stretch once a day, and add one minute a week until you work up to a full twenty minutes. If twenty minutes is too much to ask right now, just do what you can. If you would like to do more than twenty minutes, up to sixty minutes is fine. You can also break up your training into two sessions, one morning and one evening.

What you can expect: The Concentration Game usually exposes the fact that we have the attention span of a five-year-old child. If you can get to "6" without being distracted, you're already doing very well. Your skill will build over time, and you will find the exercise to be a powerful way to regain lost focus or to prepare for action.

When you play the Concentration Game, you change the way your brain functions, the chemicals that your body makes, and the way your nervous system uses energy. These physical changes translate into a sensation of being grounded, centered, and focused. As you work with the exercise, you will find your sense of self-control and patience growing, while your mind becomes more clear and present.

The Magic of Misdirection

CHAPTER | 22

Many magicians don't like performing sleight-of-hand tricks in front of children. Illusion depends on the conjurer's ability to control the attention of the audience and, as one magician friend put it, "kids don't look where they are supposed to." Ever notice that when a magician makes one object disappear, another one is produced with a flourish and a flash? That's misdirection. So are the ever-present attractive young lady in the revealing outfit and the pyrotechnics. Misdirection works best with a mind that is polite enough to look where it is directed and experienced enough to anticipate what is going to happen. Unconditioned by society and open to possibility, children tend to wield their attention, where most adults surrender it. No sooner has the magician declared a coin "vanished," then a little voice in the audience pipes up, "No it isn't! You put it in your pocket!"

Misdirection is also a major ally when it comes to mastering the Mind's First Rule. The person afraid of getting an injection looks away from the needle. The young man who attempts to control his sexual arousal tries to think of the face on the fifty-dollar bill and not his partner. What do we tell someone climbing in a high place? "Don't look down!" While we all instinctively practice misdirection, few employ it as a tool. Sudden shifts in attention radically alter Information Transduction. They release mounting tension and break up old habit patterns before they have a chance to take hold.

How can you make misdirection work for you? Longing for that second piece of cheesecake? Put some music on and dance. Thinking about having a cigarette? Go for a brisk walk. Deadlocked in negotiation with someone? Tell a joke. In pain? Catch a stand-up comedy act. Purposely pointing your attention away from the issue and toward something zany, engrossing, or *180 degrees out from what you would normally do* can give you an edge on withdrawal, ease pain, and allow some space for a solution to slip in.

Unfortunately, this kind of "creative denial" has it limits. Distraction, like stage magic, is actually an illusion, no matter how real it looks. Misdirection can take the edge off, but to move personal performance and transformation to the next level, you have to harness your imagination.

A Final Thought on Attention

C H A P T E R | 23

One day the Buddha was walking down the street when a man, noticing his enlightened radiance, came up to him and asked, "Are you a god?" "No," the Buddha replied. "Then are you a magician or a sorcerer?" the man asked. Again, "No" was the reply. Still confounded by the Buddha's power, presence, and grace, the man persisted, "Then what are you?" The Buddha answered, "I am awake!"

Attention is a remarkable tool. Attention kicks off Information Transduction and gives you great leverage when it comes to managing the First Rule. Attention is the entryway into the zone and the birthplace of higher performance and greater happiness. We have discussed several ways that you can begin to train your attention. These exercises are primers that we will build upon as we move through the Rules. Wield your attention wisely and you will never regret the effort. Surrender attention without direction, and your dreams will drift into memories and you will reside on the plateau of mediocre performance forever. You choose.

When Transcendental Meditation was first introduced in America in the 1950's, doctors lauded TM's ability to help people relax. Hearing the physicians' praise, the movement's founder, Maharishi Mahesh Yogi, shook his head and said, "I keep trying to wake you up and all you want to do is go back to sleep." The attention exercises will give you physical energy, emotional enthusiasm, and propel you toward your goals, but only if you zone *in* instead of zoning *out*. Think of the exercises as a saddle and bridle for your attention. Now, let's ride.

IMAGINATION

Why Visualization Doesn't Work

CHAPTER | 24

As a prisoner of war in North Vietnam, Major James Nesmeth spent seven years locked in a cage that was approximately four and one-half feet high and five feet long. Deprived of physical activity and comfort, and without human contact, Major Nesmeth began to *play* golf in his imagination to keep himself sane. He didn't just "visualize" a picture in his mind or think about the game, *the major played golf.* He felt the grip. He heard the club head strike the ball and the birds singing. He walked each step and imagined every detail including the clothes he wore, the fragrance of the trees, and the condition of the course.

Major Nesmeth "played" in summer sun showers and on blustery autumn afternoons. He competed against other golfers and took four hours to play eighteen holes, roughly the time it takes to play a round in the real world. Along the way Nesmeth coached himself and refined his strategy, his follow-through, and his chip shot. In his mind, each swing was perfect, no putt missed, and he never hooked or sliced a ball.

Not long after his release, Major Nesmeth returned to the United States and walked out onto a real golf course. Before his imprisonment, he had been an average weekend golfer posting scores in the mid-90s. That day James Nesmeth shot an amazing 74. While 80 percent of golfers worldwide *never* break 80, Nesmeth *imagined* his way to the front of the pack without ever swinging a club. Asked about his remarkable accomplishment, the Major quipped, "Worst game of golf I've played in seven years."

Feats like lowering your golf score by twenty points or, perhaps more important, *not* collapsing mentally in the face of extreme and cruel adversity take more than seeing little pictures in your mind's eye. The concept of visualization is a one-dimensional view of a multifaceted and extremely dynamic process. Imagine paying the full price of admission and sitting in the movie theater without the sound. Major Nesmeth integrated *all* his internal senses and basic perceptions into his imagination, not just the visual ones. He *occupied* this internal environment, not just *observed* it.

This type of deep absorption is like a session of intensive tutoring to your brain and body. Over and over, the nervous system gets the opportunity to taste perfection and integrates its experience into organismic awareness. Accuracy, power, concentration, efficient movement, or any desired emotional response literally becomes second nature, as the body learns from the imagination and then "runs with the ball."

However, this level of mind-body integration doesn't come from mental imagery alone. To accomplish the extraordinary, you will need the cooperation and collaboration from your mind's most underrated resource, the creative intelligence.

Imaginement

In the darkness of the movie theater, people are crying. The hero has died and, even though everyone knows that the actor who portrays him is actually living in Malibu and dating a supermodel, they *feel* as though they have suffered a great loss. In the next theater, hearts pound because a vicious pack of man-hunting dinosaurs is on the loose (apparently extinction isn't as permanent as was once thought). In theater three, everyone is feeling warm and cozy because in a romantic comedy, love conquers all.

How can these folks cry, fear, and laugh at events they know are not real? They suspend their rational judgment during the movie and allow the imagination to activate the body and create the emotions they feel. The same is true for the physical and emotional effects that you create at your own "Inner Cinema." Imagining a future argument, you experience anger just as if the conflict were actually happening. You see your opponent's face, hear the shouting, and perhaps even imagine a physical fight. Your pulse rate increases, your muscles tighten, and you seethe with hostility. The fact that all this is taking place only in your imagination doesn't lessen the flow of energy along the nervous system and out into the body. So it is with sexual fantasies, catastrophic fantasies, or winning-the-lottery fantasies: You *know* the images, sounds, and other imagined senses are not real, but your body and emotions respond just the same.

Unlike your attention, which you can shake up and command with hard-and-fast rules, your imagination is a relationship of *interplay*. You give up critical judgment and your imagination gives you access to unlimited possibility. Surrender control, and your imagination supplies vivid detail. Stay focused on an idea or a theme, and the imagination integrates the information directly into the nervous system. (If surrendering control is a big issue for you, skip to the Third Mind Rule for coaching on letting go.)

Obviously, you have a long history of interaction with your creative nature, but how do you know your work with the imagination is making a difference? Simple, look to your body and emotions for feedback. Images, symbols, and words that engage attention, that alter the energy level in the body, and that leave an emotional impression *will* be effective. While mastering the imagination is more art than technique, it doesn't have to be difficult. In fact, it is as easy as having a dream—a daydream.

Daydream Believer

CHAPTER | 26

It is hard to imagine, but Albert Einstein's high school report card often went home with remarks like "not working up to potential" and "serious underachiever." In addition to poor grades, Albert infuriated his teachers by sitting in the back of the room "spaced-out," half smiling, lost in a world of his own. Albert was eventually steered to a school in Aarau, Switzerland, that had a knack for reaching free-spirited dreamers. Where his old school had seen discipline and authority as the essential building blocks to learning, the Aarau school held freedom and visual imagination as the keys to unlocking the mind's potential. Albert excelled. The creative and *intentional* use of the imagination became an integral part of his thinking process. Einstein later maintained that that his best ideas first came in the form of mental images. The math and the words to explain them followed later, many times *years later.*

You don't have to be Einstein to understand how to use your imagination creatively. The recipe is simple: Take one daydream and add a sprinkle of intention and a dash of attitude. You begin the process by *consciously* mapping out your dream. *Attention* to an important personal issue and *intention* to utilize your creative function activate your imagination.

Get a piece of paper and draw out the Transduction Triangle (Chapter 5). Start in the center and work backward from Action. List a few (no more than three) of the essential outcomes you want to accomplish. If you want to smooth out your relationship with a teenage son or daughter, you might list "laugh together more," "talk together more," or "spend quality time." A competitive marksman might list "winning the tournament" or "100 consecutive bull's-eyes." Next move to Emotions. How do you want to feel? Where the parent might list "warm and relaxed," the competitor might list "confident and focused." Zero in on feeling words that accurately and powerfully represent the emotions you want to have when the Action is accomplished. (Check the feeling vocabulary chart in Chapter 55 for help finding the most potent words.)

MIND
❶ Focus on ball's dimpled surface
❷ Read The Mind Rules
❸ Play one hole at a time

ACTION
Hit longer shots on the fairway

BODY
❶ Take lessons
❷ Lift weights
❸ Swing with the whole body

EMOTION
❶ Feel in rhythm
❷ Have fun
❸ Feel like I'm doing my best

"TO BREAK EIGHTY"

After identifying the emotional responses that fit you best, move on to the Body. List the exact physical components that create the Action (remember, no more than three). The parent might note "praise them more often" or "listen more." The marksman may put down "hold breath" and "squeeze the trigger."

Once you determine the necessary movements or physical actions involved in creating your outcome, move on to the imagination. Jot down a few of the internal images and other sense impressions that represent, to you, the achievement of your goal or outcome. The parent may list a "breakthrough conversation and "smiling faces," while the tournament contender might write about "receiving the trophy" and the "roar of the crowd."

Lastly, write down one sentence that represents the basic concepts and ideas that easily convert into the internal images, physical actions, and emotional responses you previously listed. *This is the "information" that directly transduces down into the accomplishment of your ultimate goal.* Parents might list "My children are important to me and I want to understand them." The competitor might write, "Because of my hard work, excellent coaching, and great physical condition, I have everything I need to win."

While this is a rough draft that you will refine over time, your daydream storyline is essentially complete. When dealing with the imagination, take Roosevelt's advice: "Be brief, be sincere, and be seated." It is dreamtime.

Nonlinear Daydreams

CHAPTER | 27

The "map" you have just made is your ticket to the Inner Cinema. Pick a seat that is comfortable and settle in. First, use your *attention* to intensify your *intention* by studying your map. Think about why this goal is so important and focus on how each of the components contributes or relates to the outcome. See if you can concentrate on the special significance of your dream to the point where some emotions start to stir. Don't wait for huge waves of sentiment to wash over you; just let the strong ties that you have to your goal bring up some feeling energy.

When you are ready, close your eyes. Focus your attention inward on any neutral image, such as a purple rose, the number 5, or a blank white canvas (Chapter 20). After just a few seconds, imagine your map in your mind's eye and focus your attention on the top of the triangle. Silently repeat to yourself the words written on your list of concepts. Make no effort to force mental images to appear. Just focus your attention on those ideas and *let* your natural associations with this information *develop* into a daydream complete with internal images, sounds, and perceptions. Stay focused and stay involved. Daydreams differ from their nocturnal cousins *because* you remain consciously aware. Gently prompt your imagination with the information on your list and let transduction do its job.

As concepts transform into imaginary scenes, start working your way around the triangle. Move on to the body and mentally review *exactly* what you have to do to create your outcome. Focus on the physical form, movements, and actions and let that information incite your imagination. Keep the imagery flowing through internal commentary and play-by-play descriptions. "I smooth out my down stroke by keeping my eye on the ball." "I make eye contact with the interviewer as we speak." Again, let the imagination respond to the information. At this point, you may find your body getting involved. Vital signs, like breathing and heart rate, might shift, or the muscles that correspond to the images in your mind might twitch or tense slightly, indicating your nervous system is on-line and responding.

After a few moments, move on to your list of emotions. Silently repeat the words and ideas about how you want to feel when you are taking action. "When I approach the ball, I feel confident, powerful, and smooth." "During the interview, I feel poised, competent, and connected." Then let your emotions spontaneously emerge. As your daydream deepens, add more details and allow your feelings to expand. The last stop is the X on your map: Action. Imagine that your goal is already accomplished, that is, the ball drops into the hole or the audience gives you a standing ovation. Wrap your imagination around this fait accompli, and after a few moments exit your daydream by opening your eyes.

This process can take as little as a few seconds or as much as an hour, but remember, it is the consistency of your practice that counts. Five minutes every day will be much more effective that one fifty-minute session per week. Intentional daydreaming on a regular basis turns empty fantasy into an effective teaching tool for both your mind and body.

Linear Daydreams

When Joe Simpson signed on to climb Siula Grande, high in the Peruvian Andes and deep in the Third World, he knew that there would be no rescue teams or helicopters to pluck him off the mountain if disaster struck. So, when he broke his leg on top of the 21,000-foot peak, Joe was obviously concerned. When he became separated from his climbing partner and fell down a cliff face into an ice crevasse, he was certain that he was going to die. That's when "the Voice" took over.

For three horrific days, Joe's inner Voice commanded him to climb, hop, and crawl down the mountain and drag his broken body six miles over glacier and moraine to get back to base camp. When he became exhausted and started to hallucinate, the Voice jolted him back to reality by demanding, "Go on, keep going...you've wasted too much time. Move!" When he almost fell asleep in a storm, the Voice commanded, "Don't sleep, don't sleep, build a snow cave." Simpson made his way back to camp just hours before his party, thinking he was surely dead, was scheduled to leave the mountain.

Joe Simpson knows one thing for sure, when his body was beaten and he was in hopeless despair, it was the Voice that kept him alive. Like Joe, you must find your inner voice. Not the voice of reason, which tells you what you should do. Nor the voice of your conscience, telling you that you will be sorry later if you eat that second helping of ice cream now. The voice you are looking for is the voice of authority. Unlike the sardonic voice of your internal critic or the whiny voice of your inner child, the Voice *speaks through your imagination in clear tones and direct terms.* This is the "I'm gonna tell ya' how it's gonna be" side of your nature. If you put the Voice to use, your body and emotions will listen.

Diagram out your daydream using the Transduction Triangle as a guide and give it a thorough review. This time, when you close your eyes, have the curtain of your Inner Cinema open on to a blank screen. Let the Voice begin to *direct the scene* with strong, emphatic statements about you and your goal. Think documentary and let the Voice begin by outlining the five Ws: Who, What, When, Where, and Why. "I am on the golf course." "It is October 7th, the day of the championship." "I have come to play my best game and to take home the first-place trophy."

Allow the internal images to come and go as you tell your body exactly what it needs to do and tell your emotions how you will feel. After you make a strong statement such as "My whole body drives the ball" or "I am calm, alert, and feel in control," watch the corresponding inner images and senses flow in and out and notice how your body and emotions respond to the Voice. Once you have covered all the angles of the Transduction Triangle, exit the Inner Cinema by opening your eyes.

You can *demand* excellence from your mind and body. You can command change. You can do this now.

Deleting Echoes

CHAPTER | **29**

"I got you babe, pa-pa-pa-pa, I got you babe." The traffic light had given the radio just enough time to get in one more oldie. Now Sonny and Cher had climbed in my ear and were trapped in my brain. "I Got You Babe" got me. All day I caught myself humming, "They say our love won't pay the rent..." and fell asleep to the long refrain at the end, "I—Got—You—Babe." Christmas carols, advertising jingles, or worse, Barry Manilow, can all take up indefinite residence in your mind and drive you to distraction. But catchy tunes aren't the only echoes floating around in the background of your brain. Thoughts of failure, memories of mistakes, and past moments of uncertainty creep into the imagination and wreak havoc with transduction.

How do you delete these obtrusive and inhibiting ideas? Bruce Lee beat doubt by setting it on fire. Bruce gave Joe Hyams, the author of the magnificent book *Zen and the Martial Arts*, his secret for ridding the mind of negative thoughts. "When such a thought enters my mind," Lee said, "I visualize it as being written out on a piece of paper. Then I visualize myself wadding the paper into a tight ball. Then I mentally light it on fire and imagine it burning to a crisp. The negative thought is destroyed."

Bruce's imaginary ritual pulled the plug on negative information *before* it mushroomed into performance problems or robbed him of power. Interestingly, this kind of "imaginary interception" can be found in many systems of self-help. In Rational Emotive Therapy, practitioners are counseled to internally shout "No!" when they encounter a childish thought. In Neurolinguistic Programming,

71

people are told to imagine the unwanted scene like a movie running backward. I tell my clients to imagine a giant rubber stamp marking the idea with the letters WOE, for Waste Of Energy.

Does it matter what you imagine? Not really. Just select any imaginary sequence of events that symbolizes to you the elimination of the negative thought. When you encounter fear-based thinking or a recurring negative memory, run it through the grinder, shoot it off into space, or use an eraser. Then redirect your attention back to what needs to be done right now to accomplish your dream. In a few short seconds, you can take the charge out of your negative thoughts and get your transduction back on track.

What should you do with leftover holiday carols or inane song lyrics that you would like to forget? Stop struggling! *What we resist persists.* The harder you try to not to think about Frosty the Snowman, the louder the tune becomes. Get your brain to let go by being more interactive with your imagination. When you become aware of the repetitive melody, play with it: Change the beat, create a rap spin-off, unleash "Frosty the Opera," do anything but fight the jingle. Or do what I do. Call in an air strike.

Field Training

CHAPTER | 30

Speed, precision, and power depend on the fluid transfer of thought as it passes through the imagination en route to becoming energy in the body. Exercising the creative link between your mind and body increases this inner conductivity and creates a state of super-transduction, otherwise known as the zone. The following process is an expanded variation of the IT Test that you took in Chapter 11. It is the First Rule personified, and it is unsurpassed as a tool for integrating thought and action. If you only practice one skill in this book, make this the one.

FIELD TRAINING EXERCISE

It is widely believed that an energy field surrounds the human body. Whether you can really sense this field or not is unimportant. Consciously suspend your critical judgment and pretend that this bioenergetic force is not only palpable but that it is also *under your complete command.*

Start the exercise with your eyes closed. Stand or sit and turn your palms up so that they face each other about six to eight inches apart. Breathe in and relax your neck and shoulders when you exhale. First, focus inward on a neutral image for a few seconds (Chapter 20). Next, turn your attention to the energy field surrounding your hands. Tune in to the pulsing of the current as it draws the hands together and then pushes them apart. In your mind's eye, see the force take form and notice its color and sensation of power or heat. As the current increases, compress the energy between your palms down to about the size of a baseball, and then reverse it and expand the energy out to the size of a basketball. (This may sound crazy to you, but if you suspend judgment for just a moment the experience will feel quite real.) See if you can cause the intensity of the field to change by the way you breathe.

Keep playing with the energy until you feel you have established solid control and then try the exercise with your eyes open. You will notice that if your mind becomes distracted or begins to analyze or judge, the power fades. Keep practicing until you can generate the field and control the flow while your eyes are open, your body is moving, or you are talking. Then see if you can generate that power for a few moments before you take a swing or shoot a basket. Take a second to turn on your body's field generator just prior to giving an important presentation or before making love. As neural pathways form around your *intentional* use of the transduction process, actions become automatic and attitude becomes unstoppable.

COMMUNICATION

The Kansas Experiment

CHAPTER | 31

In 1976, a pioneering research project was conducted at an emergency hospital in Kansas. Paramedics were trained to utilize a series of communication procedures with emergency patients as they administered standard medical care. First, the paramedics were to remove the patient from the crowd as soon as possible to prevent the patient from hearing the negative comments often made by onlookers. Second, conversation between the paramedics unrelated to the patient or negative in nature was not to occur. Third, even if the patient was unconscious, the paramedics were to recite a memorized paragraph in a low tone, with the paramedic's mouth close to the patient's ear.

The experiment lasted six months and the results were significant. Across the board, from car accidents and heart attacks to drug overdoses and broken bones, patients had higher survival rates, shorter hospital stays, and quicker recoveries *whenever the communication procedure was used.*

What were the magic words the paramedics were taught to say? "The worst is over. We are taking you to the hospital. Let your body concentrate on repairing itself and in feeling secure. Let your heart, your blood vessels, everything, bring themselves into a state of preserving your life. We're getting you to the hospital as quickly and safely as possible. You are now in a safe position. The worst is over." These simple directives saved lives. M. Erik Wright, M.D., the internationally renowned psychologist and psychiatrist who conducted the experiment, said, "It seems absurd to find that such a relatively minor intervention could make such a difference. During the training, the paramedics themselves became the proselytizers and we had difficulty in keeping them from spoiling the experiment and teaching the others."

Words are a powerful medicine. However, since we live in a world where speech is "free," "talk is cheap," and "yada-yada-yada," few people value their words. Each time you make a statement aloud, your words must be converted into biological reactions and emotional responses that are processed by everyone within earshot, including you. As lie detector tests easily show, verbal expression not only affects the listener, but words are blitzing the speaker's nervous system as well. Words and the way you use them are either forging neural pathways to personal power or they are reinforcing the exact ideas you are trying to reject.

Information management through communication means finding the most potent and accurate words and phrases to express what you think, feel, and do. Potent words excite the imagination and accurate ones resonate with the reality of your experience. One releases energy and the other allows you to be authentic. Words reflecting power and integrity easily transduce down into desirable sensations, feelings, and actions.

The Kansas Experiment certainly wasn't the first time that doctors put the healing power of words to work. In the late 1800's, James Esdaile, a British surgeon, performed more than three thousand operations with words as the only anesthetic. Three hundred of these were major surgeries. One observer told of witnessing Esdaile remove a cancerous eye from a patient while the other eye looked on unblinkingly.

Attack of the Neutral Words

C H A P T E R | 32

Do not think of a monkey. Especially do not imagine an organ grinder's monkey in his little red vest, holding a tin cup. Do not think of a large gorilla eating a yellow banana. Whatever you do, don't think about barrels of monkeys having fun. What happened? Most likely you found that the harder you tried not to think of a monkey, the more images of monkeys appeared.

"Don't," "no," and "not" are neutral words. *Your mind does not hear them.* Instead, your attention shifts to the stronger, image-producing part of the sentence. In order *not* to think of a monkey, you have to bring up the mental image of a monkey. But "don't," "no," and "not" do more than unleash unwanted images in your imagination, they also impact your performance. The golfer who thinks, "Don't go in the water trap" or the singer who focuses on "not missing the high note," turns the tool of internal communication into an act of self-sabotage. The words create a mental image of what they don't want to have happen, which produces physical tension and programs the nervous system to respond *exactly the wrong way.*

Talking in terms of what you don't want to happen releases "No" messages into the system. "No" messages pin your mind to the mat and rob you of physical and emotional strength and power.

How do you avoid the attack of the neutral words? Use your ears. Listen for "don't," "no," and "not" when you present your ideas to people. When you hear "I don't want" statements, turn the concept around and commit to talking in terms of what you *want* to have happen. Speak about how you *want* to think, feel, and act. For example, stop talking about the first-tee jitters and start thinking in terms of poised, smooth play. Instead of focusing on not feeling afraid, state the fact that you are searching for courage. Turn anxiety around and talk about excitement.

Speaking about what you want to have happen sends out "Go" messages to the body and the nervous system. And "Go" messages work like a mind/body "high-five."

Constructive spin does much more than paint a smiley face on your problems. It creates a powerful mindset that eventually becomes a habit of thinking in terms of assets, options, and resources. Instead of wasting energy avoiding a problem, you creatively build momentum by moving toward a solution. When it comes to self-mastery, a twist to the old adage is also quite true: "Monkey speak, monkey do."

It is your choice:

"I will *not* be tense and uptight!"

Or

"I remain relaxed, poised, and focused."

Talk Isn't Cheap

CHAPTER | 33

Dr. Bernard Lown, a renowned Harvard cardiologist, witnessed an incredible incident involving a middle-aged woman hospitalized with tricuspid stenosis (TS), a non-life-threatening narrowing of one of the valves in the heart. During rounds one morning, Lown and several other doctors entered this patient's room. Her attending physician told the visiting MDs, "This woman has TS." The doctors then left the room. For some reason, the woman decided that TS meant "terminal situation." She began to hyperventilate and sweat profusely. Her pulse rate shot up to 150 beats per minute. Upon learning of her fear, her doctor tried to explain what TS meant and get her to calm down, to no avail. She died that same day.

If words have the power to heal, then it stands to reason that they can do untold harm. Many common words and phrases are actually toxic. It is likely that you used these poisonous phrases today and, through habit, you are teaching them to your children. Because you have heard or said these words so many times, they have carved the neural equivalent of the Grand Canyon through your brain and body. So, no matter what you *mean* when you use these phrases, they are still lies, blame, distortions, and excuses to the nervous system. Clean up your communication by avoiding these poisons and you *immediately* change the information you transduce.

What are the poisoned words and toxic terms? Here is a list of the most noxious:

CAN'T

Climbing on the roof, sprouting wings, and flying away is an "I can't." "I can't stop eating chocolate" or "I can't ask him out!" are actually things you *can* do, but would rather not. "I can't" sends a message of helplessness out to the world and along your nervous system.

SHOULD

"Should" is a leftover piece of the disappointed parent routine. Designed to control or manipulate behavior through guilt, "should" usually winds up transducing frustration, resentment, and self-loathing instead of the desired action.

YOU MAKE ME

"You make me" conveniently allows you to sidestep responsibility while it strips you of power.

NEED

"Need, must, have to" all belong to a group of words known as imperatives. Speaking in terms of need activates the stress response in the body and generates feelings of deprivation or desperation. Oxygen, water, food, light, love, shelter, and clothing are needs; that new car is a want.

ALL

"All, everyone, always, never, no one" are classified as absolutes. Absolutes are distortions. They magnify and exaggerate the worst in life—"I always screw up." Or they transduce into gullibility and denial—"Everyone is doing it." Combining absolutes and imperatives can be crippling. When "needs" are "never" met, the results are depressing.

TRY

Innocent in appearance, "try" implies weakness and is actually tied to failure. While it is nice to think of "try" in terms of encouragement, it is more often used as an excuse. "Try" sends the message, "Please forgive me because I am about to fail" and leaves you to face your challenge with nothing more than a doubting hope.

Turning Poison into Medicine

Acetylene burns at 3000 degrees Celsius, hot enough to vaporize an ironworker's shirt and turn his skin to charcoal. The doctor put cool towels on the charred forearm and *directed* the patient to cool down the wound and make it comfortable by imagining some form of internal cooling taking place. Even though this is a high-tech ER in Texas and the doctor in charge is a burn specialist, this patient is treated with just cool towels and words. The results are astounding. No pain medication is required. No swelling or edema, normal for this type of burn, can be seen. The man returns to work the next day! Twelve days later, the wound is completely healed. No scar tissue can be found. Dr. Dabney Ewin, a diplomat of the American Board of Surgery, expects this type of dramatic response from patients who receive his medical care and communication directives within one hour of being burned. Dr. Ewin should know; he has been successfully treating burn injuries with cool towels and mind power since 1978.

For better or worse, if you change your communication you will change your life. The antidote to the toxic terms that are running rampant in everyday language is *accuracy*. Choosing words that accurately reflect your reality allows you to have some control over the *rate* at which you transduce information. You are about seven words away from a higher life condition.

WON'T

"I won't" may seem like a small step away from "I can't," but it is a world away in meaning. "Won't" implies choice and choice indicates control. Besides, it is most often the truth. "I can't lie" is a lie. "I won't lie" is an affirmation of character and power. Feeling doubts? Then say so. "I can't do that" becomes "I'm afraid to" or "I don't think I can."

COULD

"Should" messages imply that a mistake has been made, that an opportunity was lost, and someone has failed. "Could" messages excite the ARAS and create feelings of hope and possibility. When "I shouldn't have eaten so much" becomes "I could have eaten less," you affirm the desired behavior, not the failure.

WANT

The answer to the loose use of absolutes lies in vocabulary. Words that succinctly describe your feelings, desires, and situation have power and drive Information Transduction. You take hold of this process when you chose to communicate in accurate and lucid detail about the things that are most important to you. To eliminate imperatives, you need a reality check and the words "I want." You *need* transportation. You *want* a new car. You do not "have to" lose weight or work out. Even if your weight is a life-threatening problem, there are no fitness police forcing you to diet and exercise. "I want to" makes your actions a choice.

I FEEL

"I feel" replaces "You make me" because blaming others for your transduction is like changing seats on the Titanic, a total waste of time.

I AM, I WILL, I CAN

"Try" focuses one eye on failure, which only leaves one eye to find the correct way. Once committed to a course of action, it is time to cut your ties with failure and eliminate "try" messages. Yoda said it best, "Do or do not. There is no try."

LIFE

CHAPTER | 35

In the middle of the night, a burglar is trying to crack the safe at a pet store when he gradually becomes aware that something is standing behind him. Turning around, he finds a giant Doberman Pinscher staring at him. However, since the dog's tail is wagging and he seems at ease, the thief decides to proceed with opening the safe. Suddenly a voice shouts, "Put your hands up!" Whirling around, the thief realizes that the voice belongs to a parrot. Making a mental note never to rob another pet store, the thief again tries to finish his job but the parrot won't stop squawking, "Put your hands up! Put your hands up!" Frustrated, the burglar turns to the parrot and asks, "Can't you say anything other than put your hands up?" The parrot replies, "Yea. Sic him!"

If you were given an audience with the world's most powerful computer, a machine so smart that it could answer any question you might care to pose, would you ask it, "What's wrong with me?" Would you prefer to know, "Why can't I ever catch a break?" or "Why am I such an idiot?" Questions are a direct link to the imagination and the creative function. Your mind is a goal-striving and goal-achieving machine. Put the imagination on a mission to discover your personal deficiencies and character flaws, and I guarantee you won't like the answers it returns.

Another problem with these questions is that they are not questions. They are statements in questions' clothing. Undisguised they sound like, "There is something wrong with me, tell me what it is." Or "I am an idiot, now tell me why." Based on negative assumptions and loaded with vague distortions, these statements create conflict in the nervous systems and inhibit a clean exchange of energy between the mind and body. The only thing wrong is that you are asking the wrong questions. While most people are hung up on "Why?" it is actually questions like "What if?" "How do I?" or "When?" that allow you to direct your imagination and manage information.

"If" is the imbedded question in life, and asking "What if?" kick-starts the imagination. "What" helps you to define your goals and makes them more concrete. "How" keeps your attention on the target and generates information that is *useful.* "When" puts a timeline to your dreams and plans.

"What is important to me?" "How will I accomplish it?" "When will I know that I have succeeded?" "What is my greatest resource?" "How do I hit a serve like that?" "How can we double sales?" The right questions control transduction and set the stage for higher performance. The wrong questions get you bit by a big dog.

What were you born to do?

Energy Management

Modus Operandi

CHAPTER | 36

Alice can't take her eyes off the snake. She is terrified. Her heart pounds furiously. She is shaking, crying, and perspiring. Her breathing has become so rapid that she's feeling weak and faint. She is panicked. The cold reptilian stare, the smooth skin, the thought of how fast snakes can move and bite fill her with an overpowering feeling of dread. Alice has to look away and fight against the instinct that is telling her to run for her life. Alice's panic might be understandable if she were in the presence of a real physical threat, but the snake she is looking at is *only a picture in a book*. Alice is going through desensitization therapy. Over the next four hours, she will be slowly moved from the picture book of snakes to a face-to-face meeting with a live reptile.

The First Rule has got Alice gripped, and she is not alone. Mountain climbers, professional athletes, and even media stars all have to deal with the issue of information overload. While NBA champions might not call it a "phobia," each will confess to being "psyched-out" a time or two. Adrenaline, anxiety, and intense emotion are all part of the package when you are pushing *your* envelope. As my climbing mentor once said, "All the climbers without fear died a long time ago."

When information goes biochemical, our bodies are instinctively programmed with four possible response modes for dealing with challenge and adversity. Mode One is fear. We meet adversity, overload, and freeze. This is the "Bambi" defense. Stay perfectly still and hope the problem will pass. Mode Two is sham rage, which is an intense display of aggression with no real power to back it up. Like a cat arching its back and hissing to keep other cats out of its food bowl, we puff up and show a lot of bluster but we are bluffing. In Mode Three we are not kidding any more, now we are really angry. This is rage mode. Information has transduced to pure emotion, which is driving our actions. Rage is power; even a mouse will attack an elephant if sufficiently enraged. So it is no surprise that most people learn to win by using this explosion of physical and emotional energy. After all, it works. However, the real prize is behind door number four.

Mode Four is where the body is in a balanced state of readiness and relaxation. The mind is full of intent, leaving no room for doubt, hesitation, or fear. The emotions are composed like a calm point in a whirling universe. In animals, Mode Four is called predatory attack. In humans it is called the zone.

MIND 2 MUSCLE

Wetware

CHAPTER | 37

Early in the 20th century, a young psychology student named E.B. Twitmyer conducted research on innate reflexes at the University of Pennsylvania. Twitmyer believed that the knee-jerk reflex might be influenced by the motivational state of the subject. Experimenting with fellow graduate students, Twitmyer set up a device that automatically struck the knee tendon with a small hammer, creating the knee-jerk response. When his graduate guinea pigs complained that the blow caught them by surprise, Twitmyer rigged up a warning signal to sound just before the hammer fell.

Working with a subject whose knee had been tested hundreds of times, Twitmyer accidentally gave the warning signal *without* dropping the hammer. Remarkably, the subject's leg jerked just as if it had been struck. Twitmyer had inadvertently discovered the conditioned reflex, a concept that later spawned dozens of different psychological theories and systems. The scientific establishment gave Twitmyer's findings a frosty reception, and he abandoned further research. Instead, Ivan Pavlov and his drooling dogs got credit for this monumental discovery.

Reaching the fourth mode of response, the zone, takes conditioning. From the wetware of the brain, out through the nervous system, and into the organs, muscles, and cells, neural pathways need to be created and continually refined. Smooth movement, physical power, and quick thinking depend on how well these pathways have been established, how often they are used, and how much of their flow is interrupted by the demands of other pathways or restricted by conflicts within the system, such as tension or injury. Luckily, thanks to the brain's malleable nature, known as neuroplasticity, your nervous system is a pretty quick study.

Think back to Major Nesmeth (Chapter 24). Why didn't his golf swing just dissolve after seven years of confinement with little or no physical activity? Intentionally playing imaginary golf every day kept his wetware activated and his nervous system shuttling information out to the muscles. Those muscles twitched, contracted, and expanded on cue, from the images Major Nesmeth held in his mind. You can observe this process by watching the audience at an action adventure movie. Notice how they duck, bob, and weave in response to the action on the screen? You are watching information transducing into energy.

Attention, imagination, and communication—the tools of information management—will go a long way in helping you to install and upgrade your wetware, but to build neural pathways that are bulletproof, you need to *teach* your nervous system to enter a high performance state *automatically*. Building pathways from the mind to your muscles might take a little time, but if you make a five-minute neural tune-up a regular practice, you'll be performing in the zone faster than you can say "Twitmyer."

> *The greatest thing in all education*
> *is to make the nervous system our ally*
> *instead of our enemy.*
> —WILLIAM JAMES—

The Sanford Solution

CHAPTER | 38

Rod Sanford wasn't your typical SWAT team leader. When the Santa Cruz Sheriff's Office SWAT team wanted to learn how to deal with the debilitating effects of adrenaline overload, Sanford showed them how to self-induce panic. While learning to scare yourself may sound crazy, the idea is nothing less than brilliant.

What you create, you can control. Rod's unusual solution to this Energy Management issue was to help the officers get cozy with the uncomfortable sensations of extreme stress. As the nervous system learns to work *with* this heightened biological state, it turns off the alarm bells normally associated with high-performance situations. Automatically, the mind and body become more comfortable handling these increased levels of energy. Comfort quickly translates into feelings of control, and through experimentation this sense of control evolves into mastery. Exactly how did Rod teach the deputies to avoid overload? He told them to hold their breath.

THE SWIMMING POOL EXPERIENCE

The goal of this exercise is to create the same mix of physical desperation and emotional determination that you experience when pushing yourself to swim the full length of a pool underwater and running low on air. At first this process might seem uncomfortable or even produce a slight feeling of panic, but your mind and body will quickly adapt. With just a little practice, you learn to remain relaxed and ready even under the most intense pressure.

Start in a reclined or seated position. In the beginning, keep your practice sessions short (two to three minutes) and gradually work up to longer ones (ten to twenty minutes). Begin by slowly taking in a full breath while mentally counting from 1 to 12. When you reach the number 12, hold your breath and slowly count to 3.

At 3, begin to exhale and again mentally count to 12. Coordinate your exhalation with your counting so that your lungs are empty by the time you reach the last number. Now, here comes the swimming pool part. With your lungs still empty, hold your breath and count to 3. Do not take another breath until you have completed the count. *Ride out the panicky sensations and keep control of your breathing when it comes time to take in the next breath.* On the next inhalation, start the process over again with the 12 count. Your goal is to become comfortable and controlled at each phase of the breathing cycle.

Rod Sanford no longer walks a beat, but he still fights crime and saves lives by teaching peace officers from all over the world the art of defensive tactics and the use of reasonable force. When asked, "What is the most essential ingredient to superior performance?" Sensei Sanford just smiles and says, "Patience."

When a Punch Is a Path

Without his glasses, Bruce Lee was nearly blind. To compensate, he developed fighting systems that allowed him close-quarter combat with his opponents. Because Bruce was only 5 feet, 8 inches and a lean 150 pounds, he emphasized muscle speed (velocity) rather than muscle size (mass) as the means to generate awesome power. Bruce capitalized on his limitations and developed a special technique called the "one-inch punch." Essentially, the one-inch punch is exactly that: a devastatingly powerful blow that can be delivered from as little as one inch away from its intended target. Curiously, the secret to the one-inch punch is *relaxation.*

The punch begins when you relax all the muscles in your body. Its power is released when these muscles suddenly and simultaneously snap into play. The resulting kinetic explosion is then concentrated into the fist and dumped into the target. In demonstrations, Bruce would pick a much heavier and larger volunteer and place his open hand one inch away from his subject's chest. With a movement that appeared to be no more than the closing of his fingers into a fist, Bruce Lee would send the man flying backward or knock him to the ground.

The policy of relaxation becoming power was a mainstay in Bruce Lee's martial arts philosophy. That same policy holds the key to managing the energy in your body. Consciously relaxing your body opens the lines of communication between your mental intention and the muscles, organs, and nerves that carry out the action. Over time, the simple exercise of releasing tension from the muscles *becomes* poise, power, and indestructible self-discipline. Bruce said

1 INCH PUNCH

CONCEPTS : I Relaxation
A. Antagonistic Tension

II Structure
A. Centerline
1. Linear extension Along C_L
2. Traditional or Arc Flight Paths — Greater opportunities for Energy reflux / Instability

~~Skeleton~~
B musculo - Skeletal interaction

III Physics of Impact — Energy Dumping

$$\text{Kinetic Energy } K = \frac{1}{2} m v^2 \qquad \left(\frac{d}{dt} \right)$$

~~Momentum~~

IMPULSE
Fist/Target Contact
as Time increases
K is reduced or dissipated
Back into   in the
Your Body   Target

F_{mp}
$F(t)$
$F_{external}$ (person moving Towards you, Down, Away etc)
T_i T_p
$\leftarrow \Delta t \rightarrow$

III mechanics

A. Muscles involved.
1. Increase efficiency By using other 50% of Body
2. Use of Hips

B mental
1. Focus Beyond surface

it this way, "The first step is to acquire the *feeling* of relaxation. The second step is to practice until this *feeling* can be reproduced at will. The third step is to reproduce that *feeling* voluntarily in tension-creating situations."

Like the one-inch punch, the power in relaxation must be concentrated and directed to reach its full potential. Energy Management is not just some feel-good stress-reduction exercise. The idea is to relax your muscles, not your mind, and that is where Attention, Imagination, and Communication come in. Your goal is to develop a present and focused mind in a relaxed and fluid body. Combining the tools of Information Management with the techniques of Energy Management will get you there.

> *A relaxed martial artist expends mental*
> *and physical energy constructively,*
> *converting it when it does not contribute*
> *to the solution of a problem*
> *and spending it freely when it does.*
> —BRUCE LEE—

That Magic Feeling

C H A P T E R | 40

Right now, if you wanted to, you could tense all the muscles in your body until they could not be tightened any more. This might be called the height of tension and, for most people, reaching the height of tension isn't much of a problem. But what if you wanted to release all that tension? Could you reach the "basement" of relaxation? Do you even remember where it is? Muscles have memory, which isn't a good thing when your muscles only remember how to stay in their on-guard position. To find the feeling of relaxation, it may be best to give your nervous system a lesson by way of comparison.

THE MUSCLE 2 MEMORY EXERCISE

Find a comfortable position either sitting or lying down. When you are ready, close your eyes and focus your attention inward on a neutral image (Chapter 20) such as a tree, a cloud, or an ocean wave. Hold the image in your mind for a moment and then slowly take in a full breath. As you fill your lungs with air, tense the muscles in your legs. Keep tensing the muscles in the ankles, calves, and quads as you continue to inhale. Once your lungs are full, hold your breath and hold on to the tension in your legs for three seconds. Then as you release the air from your lungs, release the tension in your leg muscles. Rest for ten seconds and focus on the feeling of relaxation. Is it a heavy feeling, a light feeling, or a tingling one? Compare the relaxation in your legs with the rest of the muscles in your body. Use the E.S.P. exercise (Chapters 17 and 18) to fully internalize all the sensations of relaxation.

After this short pause, slowly draw in another a full breath, and this time tense your upper torso and arms as you fill up your lungs.

Tighten your stomach, chest, shoulders, and back. Clench your hands into fists and tighten your arms. Hold on to the tension as you hold your breath, and after three seconds release them both. Feel the relaxation in the midsection of your body. Notice how gravity takes over. Feel the release.

On the third breath, scrunch up your face, tense your scalp, and tighten the muscles in your neck. Hold your breath as you hold the tension for three seconds, then release and relax. Notice how the face muscles relax and the jaw grows loose.

Now for the last round: *This time as you inhale, tense all the muscles in your body from your legs to your scalp.* Hold the breath and the tension to your own count of three and then exhale, release the tension, and relax all the muscles.

Repeat this last part of the process three times and then pause to let your mind and body acquire the feeling of relaxation. Soak in these sensations and let the experience of relaxation saturate your nervous system. Then open your eyes and take that relaxation with you when you get up and go.

Dynamic Relaxation

CHAPTER | 41

In 1929, long before the word "stress" became part of our daily vocabulary, Edmund Jacobson, a Chicago physician, published the book *Progressive Relaxation*. In *Progressive Relaxation*, Jacobson suggests that you cannot have the *physiological* feeling of relaxation in your body and experience *psychological* stress at the same time. This means that the habit of being chronically relaxed cancels out anxiety and, therefore, promotes emotional composure. As relaxed muscles promote the free flow of transduction, you avoid information overload and naturally enter the zone. Once again, relaxation is power!

In the previous exercise, you used the "height of tension" to reintroduce your muscles to the concept of relaxation. Now that you have gotten the feeling of relaxation, it is time to head down into the basement. Dynamic Relaxation is a twist on Dr. Jacobson's fine work. In addition to progressively releasing tension from the muscles in the body, Dynamic Relaxation allows you to deepen your relaxation to amazing levels by using your attention, imagination, and communication.

DYNAMIC RELAXATION EXERCISE

This exercise has three sections:

- Turning your attention inward

- Relaxing all the muscles in the body individually

- Deepening your relaxation through the intentional use of the imagination.

First, find a comfortable place where you can practice undisturbed for five to twenty minutes. As with all the information and energy exercises, consistent practice keeps your wetware active and your neural pathways open. While some significant additional benefits show up at about the twenty-minute mark, just five minutes on a regular basis can be extremely helpful. Recline or lie down, keeping each part of your body supported and your arms and legs uncrossed.

When you are ready, close your eyes and draw your attention inward by focusing on a neutral image or by concentrating on your breathing (Chapter 21) for a few moments. This time, skip the tension phase and move right into the relaxation. Focus your attention on your feet and progressively relax all the muscles in your legs. Work in groups of threes: feet, ankles, calves, pause while they respond; proceed to knees, thighs, hips.

Next, relax the stomach, solar plexus, and chest. Take your time and really experience the relaxation. Then relax your lower back, middle back, and broad muscles in your upper back. Move your attention over your shoulders, arms, and hands and relax them. Last, relax your scalp, forehead, and face.

Once you have relaxed your entire body, let your attention find a seat in your Inner Cinema. On the screen, imagine yourself standing at the top of a magnificent staircase. The staircase has one hundred steps. Tell yourself that as you walk down the stairs, "each step will take me deeper into relaxation…" As you imagine yourself walking down the stairs, mentally count each one. Keep releasing tension as you imagine your movement down the stairs. Keep counting and relax each muscle from the tips of your toes to the top of your head.

When you feel that you have reached the basement of relaxation and cannot relax any further, stop and notice what number stair you are on. With practice it will take fewer and fewer stairs to get you to the "basement." Relax this way for a few moments. Then exit the process by opening your eyes. Practice this exercise until you can sense the very deepest levels of relaxation and then *take* yourself there.

Does That Ring a Bell?

CHAPTER | 42

Let's go back to the Twitmyer Principle (Chapter 37) for a moment. What caused the student's leg to move even when the hammer didn't strike his knee? A bell. What caused Pavlov's dogs to salivate? A bell. What caused you, when you were a child, to run around like a nut screaming "The ice cream man is coming?" Bells. Even if it was music played through a loudspeaker instead of a bell, it is the same principle. A signal activates your wetware, which sends a message out through the nervous system and triggers a response in your body.

If you can teach your muscles *what* to do, that is, relax, then you can teach them *when* to do it. You are going to install a link between your mind and your muscles. *These links are words or phrases that shortcut the Dynamic Relaxation process and move you from tension to total relaxation in less time that it takes to read this sentence.* These word-signals work with the same trigger system as Twitmyer's bell. When you think or say this word-signal, it triggers your conditioned response, which in this case is relaxation.

I use the word "relax," but you could use words like "release," "let go," or "cheeseburger." The word-signal can have meaning, like "power down," or it can just be a sound, like "cowabunga." Golfers gravitate to words like "smooth," while a professional rodeo rider signaled his nervous system as if he was talking to a horse, saying "Whoa, whoa, whoa." A woman dealing with pain triggered her relaxation by using the word "peace." Find words that have impact and that feel right to you. And use the Voice (Chapter 28). This is a *directive* to the nervous system, not a prayer. Start the exercise with the expectation that your body can and will respond whenever you give it the signal.

RELAX AND RING

First, select a word-signal that will work like Twitmyer's bell. Then, completely relax your body with the Dynamic Relaxation process. This time when you have reached the bottom of the "staircase," use the Voice. Silently repeat your word-signal in your mind several times. Don't try to make anything happen. Just feel the relaxation and repeat the signal. Then, in your own words tell the nervous system, "Anytime I say [your signal here], my body will relax."

Run through this process several times and, when you are ready, exit the exercise by opening your eyes. Practice with this exercise until you can go through the steps automatically. How will you know that your nervous system got the signal? Simple, you are going to test it.

The Rope Trick

C H A P T E R | 43

We are 700 feet up and the rope is stuck. It has slipped down into a crack between the rocks and become wedged under a "flake" of granite. Until today, my rock climbing experience has been with short climbs or what is known as sport climbing. This ascent is what climbers call a multipitch route and, at the end of the day, we will finish at about 1,500 feet "off the deck." Up to this moment, everything has been going smoothly. Now the rope is stuck and that slight edge in the voice of my climbing mentor, Mike Ferry, tells me we are in trouble. Big trouble.

This realization quickly activates the First Rule, and it is only seconds before I am breathing in hard, short gasps like a winded sprinter in a 100-yard dash. My knees are shaking like a bobbin on a sewing machine, and my hands grip the rock ten times tighter than needed. I am starting to feel weak. That's when I become aware of the Voice. Like Obi Wan Kenobi urging Luke Skywalker to "use the force," my inner voice is telling me to use my relaxation technique. As I take a deep breath and exhale, I think to myself the word "relax" and *instantly* my muscles relax, my mind becomes clear; I let go of my fear.

Relaxation enables my body to be more flexible and have greater extension. I can now work myself down into the crack a little farther, and the half-inch reach I gain allows me to hook my foot under the rope and flick it out from under the rock. The rope is now free, and we can complete the climb. Knowing how to relax made me a hero.

RING THAT BELL

Once you have the feeling of relaxation and have created a mind-to-muscle link, it is time to put the process to the test in the real world. Start in a *challenge-free* environment, such as sitting in your living room in front of the television. When you want to relax, close your eyes and take in a full breath. When you exhale, mentally repeat your signal and *let* your body naturally respond. When you have trained your nervous system well enough, the process feels completely automatic and remarkably empowering. Next, try a more challenging venue such as standing in line at the bank or grocery store. Again, breathe in and think the signal as you exhale. This time, when you give yourself the signal, keep your eyes open. See if you can use the signal to generate a sharper mental focus and solid physical relaxation when you are active and out in public.

Once you can produce the feeling of relaxation at will in these settings, the next step is to assess your ability in tension-creating situations. Please note: You do not have to rock climb or run with the bulls in Palermo to test your response. Asking your boss for a raise, playing in the club tournament, dating, or any situation that normally elicits tension in you will do. The steps are simple: Step up to the plate, breathe in, think the signal as you exhale, and relax into power.

When you can relax your muscles in the middle of adversity, you are demonstrating self-mastery, not just talking about it. Welcome to the world of real Energy Management.

FUEL, REST, ACTIVITY

Needs

CHAPTER 44

Winston Churchill's love of food and alcohol was immense and his loathing of exercise is legendary. Five feet, six inches, and 210 pounds, Churchill consumed large, fat-laden, meat-dominated meals, often chased down breakfast with a scotch and soda, and smoked ten cigars a day. He slept less than six hours a night, was a workaholic, and at times had a raging temper. Churchill lived to be ninety-one. He was prime minister of England, saved the world from the Nazi peril, won a Nobel Prize in literature, and was a heroic giant to people on every continent. His renown was so great that in 1964, a nine-year-old girl in South America sent a card to Churchill. Without stamps and addressed only "To the Greatest Man in the World," the handmade card reached England in time for his ninetieth birthday.

Churchill also struggled with depression, suffered from bouts of pneumonia and heart aliments, and had a lackluster sex life. Normally a natty dresser, Churchill wore loose fitting, one-piece coveralls and shoes with zippers to compensate for the discomfort of his physical girth whenever possible. Sir Winston might not have accomplished much more by eating better, drinking less, and exercising, but he could have dramatically improved his quality of life.

Not many of us smoke and drink our way to the top, and Churchill is obviously an exception. To function optimally, your body needs the right quality and quantity of food, exercise, and rest. *The foods that you use as fuel, your level of physical activity, and the amount of quality rest that you get help you to manage physical energy.*

Which diet and exercise program "really" works? The truthful answer is: None of them and all of them. Every plan works for someone, and no single plan works for everyone. Search from the Atkins diet to the Zone diet and from Aerobics to Yoga, but when it comes to meeting your body's needs, systems don't work, you do. The program that you will actually follow is the one that you build yourself.

Like the rest of life, this process starts with high-powered information. Become eclectic. Study a variety of eating and fitness programs and don't be afraid to mix, match, and measure. Mix the elements from different programs that match your individual needs and measure your progress. Keep the parts of the programs that fit you and that are effective. Then discard the rest.

Most important, choose eating plans and exercise routines that you will actually do. Forget perfection and find what works for you. Winston did.

> *I get my exercise being a pallbearer for those of my friends*
> *who believe in regular running and calisthenics.*
> —WINSTON CHURCHILL—

Fuel

CHAPTER | 45

It was a packed house at the Oakland City Woman's Club. Noted health expert Paul Bragg was lecturing, and the only two chairs left for a late-arriving mother and son had to be placed on the stage near the speaker. Sickly and covered in pimples, the fifteen-year-old was mortified to be in front of so many people but was desperate enough to stick it out. As Paul Bragg spoke, Jack LaLanne transformed. Once again, information worked its magic and transduced a revolution. In this case it was the fitness revolution, and Jack LaLanne was its "godfather."

For more than three decades, *The Jack LaLanne Show* inspired millions of television viewers to "look better, feel better, and live longer" through proper nutrition and exercise. He sold the nation on the value of vitamins, and he is the role model for every personal trainer in existence today. A billboard for his beliefs, Jack swam, with his hands and feet shackled, towing seventy boats with seventy people for over a mile and a half in the Pacific Ocean for his seventieth birthday. At nearly ninety years old, he can still do fingertip push-ups. To Jack, food is fuel and exercise is medicine.

When it comes to fueling your body, three maxims stand out no matter what diet plan you study.

FOOD MAXIM #1: CHOOSE "CLEAN" FOODS
Clean foods are foods high in nutritional value: closest to their natural state, free from chemical additives, and prepared without heavy grease or excess fat. Clean foods are easily assimilated and give your body the fuel it needs to convert ideas into physical

energy. Glucose, a byproduct of the foods you take in, is gasoline for your brain. When your internal gas gauge is on "E," the fuel lines are clogged, or the octane level is wrong, transduction sputters to a grinding halt. A brain on empty results in clouded thinking, disintegrating muscular coordination, and feelings of frustration, doubt, and depression. You wouldn't run a high-performance automobile on kerosene, so how can your body perform at its peak if you fuel it with junk?

FOOD MAXIM #2: SIZE MATTERS

Gravity isn't the only law of physics that applies to your body. Like any system, if you put in less fuel than you use, the energy needed to run the system has to come from somewhere. In your body, the energy comes from stored fat. Eat less and be more active and you *have* to lose weight. Eat at the balance point between your intake and output, and you maintain your weight. Work out hard, eat slightly more, and build muscle. Forget the fad diets; the solution is actually quite simple. Practice portion control. Use a measuring cup or scale to dole out your food for one week and you might be surprised at what a six-ounce or eight-ounce serving really looks like.

FOOD MAXIM #3: EAT

Drastic diets, "empty" calorie foods, and long periods between meals trigger the body's Vigilance Reaction. Starved for nutrition, your body begins to believe that you are facing a famine and immediately goes to work storing fat, retaining salt, and suppressing sex hormones. In an effort to preserve your life, your body burns muscle, retains water, and shuts down your sex drive. The survival system that helped our ancestors make it through drought and hard times will cause you to look and feel awful. Eating clean foods, in the quantities that are right for you, will bring your body into balance and set you up for some great transduction.

Rest

CHAPTER | 46

It is not your imagination. Life *is* accelerating and becoming more complex. Pioneers in a stagecoach took six *months* to make the journey from the East coast to the West. Steam locomotives cut that travel time down to six *days*. Today, airliners make the 3,000-mile trip in less than six *hours*. The same quantum leaps have taken place in the media, medicine, and technology. In addition to increasing speed, our world is also becoming steadily more complex. What started as a covered wagon with wheels, powered by a horse, has evolved into a flying hotel propelled by jet.

Your brain loves all this. It is a stimulation junkie. From go-fast drugs like coffee and sugar to going fast on the freeway and feeding on a media smorgasbord, your brain has the urge to surge. This leaves the rest of your body to pick up the tab. While the brain fiddles, the body burns, and it is starting to show. One-third of the population has frequent or constant insomnia. Another 10 percent of Americans take over-the-counter cold or pain medications just to slow down enough to get to sleep. Chronic muscular tension is an indication that something is out of balance in your nervous system, but most people accept it as a way of life. What can you do to get the rest you need in a world that continues to pick up momentum? You are already practicing.

The Information and Energy Management skills we have covered are extremely effective in helping you to get to sleep, to stay asleep, and to *discharge stress and tension before they have a chance to accumulate and cause trouble.* Because they change the way you use your brain,

The Mind Rules exercises migrate into every aspect of your life. Dynamic Relaxation is no exception. The relaxation and poise you create to compete on the fairway naturally transfer to the traffic jam on the freeway. The deep relaxation and composure you develop for use in the boardroom will automatically find its way into the bedroom. When it comes to Information Transduction, the old sailing axiom rings true, "All boats rise with the tide." However, if you would like to take a more direct approach, the next chapter offers two exercises that will help you get the relaxation and comfort you want, as well as the high-quality sleep you need.

Relaxing into Sleep

CHAPTER | 47

Sleep is a natural process known to every organism. Even flowers enjoy some downtime. Most of the 60 million people who find it difficult to sleep think that they are suffering from insomnia. Their problem is actually information based; the information they are transducing is blocking the body's natural movement into the sleep state. They cannot get to sleep, or get back to sleep, because they are too busy worrying. I suggest that you stage a preemptive strike and *pre-worry*. Really, I want you to worry, but this time to do it hours before you go to sleep, at a designated place that is anywhere but in your bed or bedroom.

First, select a worry spot and set a time limit for how long you have to worry. Then go to that place and worry all you want. Exaggerate, amplify, and awfulize yourself into a tizzy. When your time is up, make a commitment to leave your worry there. Later, if you catch yourself lying in your bed mulling over your issues, *stop* and remind yourself that you have been there, done that, and have the bumper stickers, baseball caps, and t-shirts.

Start your descent into the sleep state way before your head touches the pillow. Slow your brain and body down by limiting your information intake one hour before bedtime. As we talked about in the Information Diet (Chapter 15), especially avoid ingesting information stimulants, like news and entertainment, right before the lights go out.

Once you are ready to go to sleep, close your eyes and begin the process of focusing inward (Chapter 20). After you have turned your attention inward for a few seconds, relax your body using Dynamic Relaxation (Chapter 41). *Your goal is only relaxation; to sleep or not to sleep is not the question.* With very little practice, just your intention to relax will immediately send you off to dreamland.

World Stopping

CHAPTER | 48

Everyone has a stress vessel. Some vessels have the volume of a 10,000-gallon tank, while others have the capacity of a teacup. In either case, once they are full, they overflow. Discharging tension from the body enhances transduction and brings the nervous system back into balance. Periodic stress purging prevents your internal vessel from filling up and spilling over in the form of chronic tension and sleep issues. Remember, about 40 percent of your body mass is skeletal muscle. Constant tension inhibits transduction and burns up your daily allotment of energy. Delete the tension and you will naturally step into greater composure, power, and focus.

Once you become skilled with instant relaxation (Chapters 42 and 43), World Stopping can be done in just a few minutes. Pick times of the day when you want to take a short break. Quickly bring up the feeling of relaxation and turn your attention inward. In the Inner Cinema of your imagination, allow the screen to open to a scene of the earth spinning in space. Imagine that the globe is slowing down and coming to a stop. Imagine a busy city street with traffic and pedestrians moving in slow motion and the sound fading and going silent. Imagine a clock that has stopped.

Now imagine the clock hands moving counterclockwise as if you were buying back time. Move the people and cars on the street in reverse and have the globe rotate backward. Now let your muscles relax fully and imagine yourself growing younger, your body rebuilding, repairing, and getting stronger. Continue to relax your muscles and, when you are ready, exit the process by opening your eyes.

Use whatever images you like, but in your mind slow everything down. A dentist who used The Mind Rules to control pain imagined himself floating in timeless weightlessness while scuba diving. A stockbroker imagined a raging river transforming into a peaceful stream. One ingenious young woman gave her nervous system a double shot of conditioning by imagining skiing down a steep run *in super slow motion.*

Since your nervous system responds to both reality and fantasy, put it to work. Relax your body and direct your perception of time. Transduce images that say to your body "Slow down." Then take that relaxation out with you into your world.

Activity

CHAPTER | **49**

Early in 2001, researchers at Duke University Medical Center made a startling discovery. They found that a supervised exercise program was as effective as a widely prescribed antidepressant medication. Diagnosed with major depressive disorder, the patients in the study attended a 40-minute workout session of brisk cycling, jogging, or walking three times a week. After sixteen weeks in the program, the patients reported that exercise brought them just as much relief as the popular pill. Six months after the study, the patients who continued to exercise continued to benefit.

Your body is an on-demand system. Ask it for very little and that is what you will get. Demand higher performance, greater strength, or better endurance, and your body will respond. Everybody's body improves with demand. Ninety-year-olds who lift weights increase muscle mass and strength, and AIDS patients who exercise regularly fare better in their fight against the disease. It was demand, in the form of commitment and training, that broke the four-minute mile. Demand, however, has diminishing returns. Overtraining is stress, as far as your body is concerned, and the outcome of overdoing it is exactly the same: you actually age faster. If every workout is a race, you won't be in the running very long. *Exercise should give you energy and build power.*

So, how do you find the level of demand that is perfect for you? Think FID. FID stands for Frequency, Intensity, and Duration. How many times a week will you work out (Frequency)? How hard will those workouts be (Intensity)? How long will each workout last (Duration)? The key to finding your FID is hidden in your goals.

From marathon runners looking to make the Olympic squad, to new moms who want to lose a few pounds, everyone's training strategy revolves around FID. FID revolves around real life. Committing to walking after work each day during summer is one thing, but how will you with deal with the short days and chilly afternoons of winter? Since time is the key element in the workout equation, people who are successful in the world of fitness are those who plan their workouts and then work their life into that plan.

Formulating your FID isn't difficult, but there are a number of factors to consider and several calculations to follow. This is where the Olympic athletes have an edge over the everyday moms: They have a coach and a trainer that figures out their FID for them. If a personal trainer isn't in the cards right now, then I suggest that you take H.E.A.R.T. Heart-rate-specific Exercise with Aerobic Resistance Training is the brainchild of fitness revolutionary Jay Williams, Ph.D. Her highly acclaimed book, *The 24-Hour Turnaround,* is packed with powerful information about the proper care and feeding of the physical body. With Jay's H.E.A.R.T. Workout Formula, you will become your own personal trainer and get your FID working for you in no time.

As I turn you over to Jay's competent hands, I ask that you remember: *Activity is a key element in Energy Management and Information Transduction.* Training at the perfect intensity level keeps your body balanced and your brain working on optimal.

Walk This Way

CHAPTER | 50

Lance Armstrong recovered from testicular cancer that had spread to his lungs and brain and went on to win the Tour de France six times. Winston Churchill returned from the obscurity of Parliament's "back bench" to lead England as prime minister during World War II. Life may be full of setbacks, but in the long run, it is the comebacks that matter. The same is true for your nervous system.

While it may be hard to imagine, stress is actually good for you. In fact, your body is designed to thrive in stressful situations, *as long as those situations are short lived.* Stress only becomes a killer when you can't break free from its grip and you spend a prolonged period of time in the fight-or-flight state. In reality, *acute* stress, such as facing a job interview or going out on a first date, actually builds you up, where *chronic* stressors, such as traffic, family problems, or financial woes, tend to break you down. This means that the faster you can get out of fight-or-flight and back into balance, the better. The secret to beating the debilitating effects of stress lies in teaching your nervous system to quickly *bounce back* from a high-energy event.

STRESS RECOVERY TRAINING
The next time you go for a walk or a run, take a bike ride, or swim a few laps, don't just work your legs, arms, and lungs, work out your nervous system. Artificially elevating your heart rate through exercise simulates the stress state. Each time during your workout that you elevate your heart rate to about 60 to 75 percent of your maximum, and then allow your pulse to return to a lower or near-resting rate, you are teaching your body to recover from stress. If you

walk at the exact same heart rate for your entire workout, you are only building in one of these beneficial recovery cycles. However, if you mimic fight or flight and allow your body to recuperate several times during your training, you will establish a faster and more efficient recovery rate. Think of this as interval training for the both the brain and body.

Start easy and warm up. Once you are ready, take your heart rate up to the point where your breathing begins to be labored and where you begin to become aware of the physical strain. Keep your heart rate up and stay in this simulated stress state for two minutes. Control your breathing, maintain calm, and keep focused during this two minute fight-or-flight interval. Like the Swimming Pool Experience (Chapter 38), you are conditioning your nervous system to associate comfort with a high-energy state.

At the end of the stress interval, build in the recovery phase by slowing down your activity and letting your body return to a steady, more relaxed pace. Intersperse a few of these intervals into your regular workouts as best fits your needs and physical ability. Your body will love you for it.

IMAGYMNATION

Imagymnation

CHAPTER | 51

The sign at the trailhead cautioned hikers that mountain lions occasionally roamed the hills of Big Sycamore Canyon. Trail running had become a "religious" experience for me, and I had come to take a long lope on the ridgeline overlooking the Pacific Ocean. I had dismissed the mountain lion warning sign many times before, but today, as I set my watch and started my run, its image stuck in my mind.

Please understand, I have had a few close encounters with cougars and bears, so I am not cavalier about the possible danger. I knew that the element of surprise would work against me in this setting. Worse, running is considered prey behavior to a cat, so one may chase you down simply on instinct and not out of hunger. The good news is that human beings apparently don't smell or taste very appealing to most predators and, given a choice, these creatures would rather just go their own way.

That being said, I took off running with thoughts of mountain lions and mountain lion attacks on my mind. These ideas quickly captivated my imagination, and after just a few minutes on the trail, my Inner Cinema was ablaze with images of full-on, no-holds-barred battle scenes between some large cat and myself. In these imagined encounters, I capitalized on the weakness I perceived in the feline's fighting strategy and pressed my advantage whenever possible. The effect that this kung fu fantasy had on my body was magnificent; I crashed through creeks and flew over hills with power and grace. As my body slipped into predator mode (Chapter 36), I felt lean, fast, and strong. I was keenly aware of and fully connected to what I was doing even while the imaginary sparring matches whirled in the back of my mind. Roaring to a finish, I was stunned to realize that I had taken over 20 minutes off my previous personal record!

For the next year and a half, four times a week I thundered through those hills with a chimerical herd of wild horses or swooped low over the meadows with imaginary red tail hawks. The images might have been all in my head, but their effect was physical; my times greatly improved and the immense feelings of personal power that were transduced during the run stuck with me long after the workout ended.

Intentionally activating the imagination during physical exercise is your shortcut to the zone. For reasons we will explore in the Second Rule, physical activity gives you direct access to your nervous system. Think back to Hank Aaron's technique for hitting home runs; he "slowed the ball down and made it bigger." Hank married imagination and movement, and the history books recorded the results. Intentionally involve your imagination in your next workout, and you will bring out the best your mind and body have to offer.

Religion: re·lig·ion (rĭ-lĭj´en) noun from Latin religio, religion—meaning to reconnect

The Imagymnasium

CHAPTER | 52

Early in his career, funnyman Bill Cosby did a standup comedy routine about the importance of having "personal" theme music as a child. Cosby preferred the theme from the *Green Hornet* radio show, while his friend opted for the opening music to the *Lone Ranger,* the "William Tell Overture." As they ran or biked through the neighborhood, they hummed or mouthed the music to add depth and excitement to their playtime experience.

Integrating imagination and movement is not difficult. Simply start moving your body and bring up a scene in your imagination that transduces into physical and emotional power. The missing ingredient for most adults is *intention to use their creative intelligence.* Stop distracting yourself by watching TV, listening to talk radio, or reading magazines during your workouts. Exercise isn't boring, you are. Cut down on the small talk when you train with partners and knock off the chitchat with your coach. It is time to engage your mind while you move your body.

INTEGRATING IMAGINATION AND ACTIVITY

Although this process seems to work best with aerobic exercises like walking, running, biking, and swimming, or vigorous sports like skiing or tennis, any type of physical activity will do. Herb Ju, a true master of the Chinese martial arts, had his class imagine their arms as charged fire hoses while practicing the T'ai Chi forms in extreme slow motion. So, it is not out of the question to imagine a rocket-powered golf ball screaming down the fairway before a shot or muscles made of steel while you lift weights.

Before you begin your activity, make a conscious commitment to stay focused and to get the most out of yourself by engaging your imagination while you are in action. Now, turn your attention outward (Chapter 17). Use your attention to absorb your environment and step into the present. As your senses become more acute, narrow your attention down and focus on what you are doing. At the same time, tap into an image, a memory, or a fantasy of success, conflict, or challenge. Let the fantasy take shape in the back of your mind, and seek out ways to enhance its strength and effectiveness.

As these images and ideas start to energize your body and stir up your emotions, allow your imagination to run free. No matter how wild, focus on the metaphors that move your mind and gravitate to the symbols that get the point across to your nervous system. The face of the tennis racket may not be two feet wide, and a powerful wind that propels you forward as you run may not actually exist, but imagine they are and watch what happens to your performance. Sexual thoughts, images of past or future challenges and confrontations, or the right music or song lyrics may be imaginary, but they will be converted into real energy.

Work out in the Imagymnasium and you win in two ways: These *activated* ideas not only fuel your body, they also forge new neural pathways and teach your nervous system how and when to respond. Your creative intelligence is simultaneously mentoring both your brain and your body through this fusion of imagery and movement. Marrying imagination and activity makes finding your way into the zone child's play.

Emotion Management

THE FEELING WAVE

The Feeling Wave

CHAPTER | 53

On May 29th, 1953, a New Zealand beekeeper and his Sherpa teammate became the first men to walk on the roof of the world. Conquering Mount Everest put Sir Edmund Hillary's face on New Zealand's five-dollar bill and made Tenzing Norgay a national hero in India, Nepal, *and* Tibet.

Hillary had this to say about fear: "I found fear a very stimulating factor. I'm sure the feeling of fear, as long as you can take advantage of it, can make you extend yourself beyond what you would regard as your capacity. If you can summon up your determination and motivation to overcome your fear, you seem to have more *energy* to tackle the problem and overcome it." Considering the fear factor inherent in climbing a 29,000-foot peak, Sir Edmund Hillary must have had enough energy to light up Broadway.

All emotions, not just fear, are energy. As energy, the power of emotion can be put to use. You can learn to work with this energy and ride the Feeling Wave. Like waves in the ocean, feelings are the byproduct of many elements. Wind, tides, and earthquakes make ocean waves, while ideas, body chemistry, and behaviors create their emotional counterpart. Just as no one can control Mother Nature, emotional tsunamis will arise in your life. Rather than trying to avoid them, work with the Mind Rules and put your feelings to use. Even when you come into contact with disturbing information, your body chemistry is off, or your performance is disappointing, you can still catch the Feeling Wave if you understand the nature of emotions and how they fit into the Mind's First Rule.

Surfing the Feeling Wave

CHAPTER | **54**

Here are some facts about feelings that aren't all wet.

YOU CAN'T CONTROL THE OCEAN

Some days the surf conditions are glassy and the waves are perfect. Other days the ocean is trashing around like a washing machine and it is a constant fight to catch a ride. Sometimes the waves are so small and slow that it is hardly worth getting wet. *The pros can surf them all.* You have to surf the waves that you get. Even if you master all the other facets of Information Transduction, you can't control your feelings. You must grow to a point where you can use your emotions as a guiding influence, a processing facility, and a source of power.

FIGHTING THE OCEAN IS A WASTE OF ENERGY

Surfers work with the ocean's tides and currents and try not to put themselves in direct opposition to the natural forces they encounter. Don't fight your feelings. The more you try to block out or deny the feelings you feel you shouldn't have, the harder they hit you back. Flow with your feelings by accepting them just as they are. Ocean or emotion, it is the same—the harder you struggle, the quicker you sink.

THE TIDE COMES AND GOES

Feelings are like the tides, they come in and they go out in natural cycles unless some force, like a storm, stirs them up. Unless you do something to agitate them, *all* feelings fade with time. Loving feelings are lost if you don't do something to stimulate your relationship, and grief dissipates if you don't constantly focus attention on your loss. Like a wave that builds, crests, and then collapses, feelings well up, hit a high point, and release at the end. Understanding this sequence allows you to hold on and not get swept away or drowned by your emotions. Recognizing that every good wave will come to an end keeps you paddling for the next ride.

WHEN THE WATER IS COLD, WEAR A WETSUIT

Wetsuits give you a protective barrier when the water is cold or chilly. Personal boundaries keep you from becoming enmeshed in the emotions of others. Just as you can remove your wetsuit and come into direct contact with the water if you want to, personal boundaries can be lowered when it is appropriate to do so. Personal boundaries are woven from the fabric of ego strength and a striving to *understand* others, rather than *feeling for* them. Empathy makes a great wetsuit, while sympathy leaves you out in the cold.

NEVER FLOUNDER AROUND LIKE A WOUNDED SEAL

Think, feel, and act like an emotional victim and sharks will find you.

IT IS NATURAL TO FALL
WHEN YOU ARE PUSHING THE ENVELOPE

Risk pays its dividends and exacts its price in emotions. Learning to use failure and regret as lessons isn't easy; it's just the right thing to do. Legendary waterman Phil Edwards was once asked how someone could learn to surf better than he did. He replied, "Easy, just surf one more wave than I have." The most valuable commodity in dealing with your emotions is life experience.

POWER WORDS

The Rumpelstilskin Factor

CHAPTER | 55

Rumpelstilskin is the story of a beautiful girl who gets into a bad business deal with a magical dwarf because of her father's big mouth. Looking to climb the social ladder, the father tells the king that his daughter can spin straw into gold. Of course, the girl can do no such thing! So when the king locks her in a room with a ton of straw and promises to kill her if she doesn't transform the hay into gold by morning, the girl has to promise the dwarf her first-born child if he will do the job. The straw becomes gold and, in a fairy tale version of the Stockholm syndrome, the girl marries the king. A year after the girl's baby is born, Rumpelstilskin returns to collect his pay but winds up taking pity on the young queen and gives her one last chance to keep her baby. If she can guess his name in three days, she wins. On the last day, a royal messenger tells the queen that he spied a dwarf in the deep forest singing a song that ended in the refrain, "Rumpelstilskin is my name." When the manikin comes for the child, the queen calls out his name, and Rumpelstilskin becomes so furious that he stomps one foot into the ground and tears himself in two trying to pull it out. This happens every day in counseling sessions.

Like the queen's messenger, good counselors help clients to find the words to fit the feelings they have and the feelings they want to have. *These power words liberate energy and unshackle transduction.* Power words help clients tear away the rigidity of their thinking. When a client says that he is "mad" because his relationship ended when he was "dumped" for someone else, the counselor feeds back more *accurate and potent* words such as "betrayed and abandoned," and an energy shift takes place. Beyond their ability to identify true feelings and provide you with better information to transduce, words are the valves that amplify or tame your emotional energy. Because words unleash ideas and concepts, it is important for you to understand that *the words themselves contain power.* Politicians, professional speakers, and advertisers move people with power words, even when they do not have an actual message. Since words contain power, knowing what they are and how to use them is power.

Below are some examples of feeling words. The top line gives you the category and the sidebar refers to varying degrees of intensity. Match the right intensity with the right category and you have your "Rumpelstilskin." In the next week, strive to use more power words in your everyday communication. When expressing your emotions to others, be accurate and descriptive. When giving feedback, make an effort to find words that accurately fit the feeling category and intensity level of the other person. Hit the feeling mark and watch how the right word alters the flow of energy within you and around you.

FEELING WORDS CHART

Levels of Intensity	Category of Feeling						
	HAPPY	SAD	ANGRY	SCARED	CONFUSED	STRONG	WEAK
HIGH	Excited Elated Overjoyed	Wrecked Devastated Destroyed	Furious Seething Enraged	Terrified Afraid Threatened	Hopeless Trapped Troubled	Powerful Super Potent	Defeated Impotent Empty
MEDIUM	Cheerful Up Pleased	Depressed Upset Sorry	Agitated Frustrated Irritated	Nervous Uneasy Insecure	Disorganized Lost Mixed Up	Energized In Command Capable	Helpless Incapable Vulnerable
LOW	Satisfied Content Good	Blue Low Bad	Annoyed Uptight Tense	Timid On Edge Unsure	Awkward Uncomfortable Undecided	Confident Sure Solid	Shaky Unsure Distracted

Say the Word

CHAPTER | 56

Power words do not need to have content, or be in context, in order to produce an effect on your emotions. Your previous experience and association with these words is so strong that they do not need any additional information to back them up. Here is a process that will put you into direct contact with the inherent power of words. This exercise works with the same principle that many actors use to "create" emotion on stage or for the camera (Chapter 9). Your goal is to find the power words that resonate with you.

PERSONAL POWER WORDS

From the list of feeling words below, or using some of your own, select two or three words that you like or that you feel fit your situation best. Any word, even "yes" or "no," can be a power word, as long as that word is meaningful to *you*. Once you have compiled your list of favorites, find a comfortable place where you won't be disturbed and get started.

Focus your attention inward (Chapter 20) and dynamically relax your body (Chapter 41). When you reach the "basement" of relaxation, silently repeat one of the power words from your list. If the word you chose is "peace," silently repeat "peace, peace, peace" and let the word sink into your nervous system. Notice how the word affects you mentally, physically, and emotionally. Try the word on and see how well it fits. If the power word creates peaceful images and peaceful memories, and you experience peaceful sensations and emotions in your body, you have a winner. If not, move down your list until you discover the word that reaches your nervous system with the most intensity or best embodies the emotions you are seeking to create.

Once you have found a word that generates the response that you want, turn it into a signal. Just as a word-signal helped you to relax instantaneously (Chapter 42), this power word will help you to manage your emotional energy. Stay focused, remain relaxed, and repeat your power word silently to yourself. As the emotion begins to form, tell your nervous system, "Whenever I say the word [your power word here], I will be [your power word (s) here]." Example: "Whenever I say the word peace, I will be clear, calm, and strong."

After you have walked through this exercise a few times, take the technique out into the world. *Without* going through the relaxation process or closing your eyes, say your power word and see if you can bring up the desired emotion. Start practicing your power word workout in nonchallenging situations. *Two prime times to practice are when you are in the shower or just before bedtime.* Once you can give yourself the signal and generate an emotional response in these settings, it is time to up the ante. Start using your power word when speaking in public, during a conflict, or in any situation in which you want to direct your emotional energy.

Once your nervous system gets into the habit of responding to your signal, all you need to do is "say the word and you'll be free."

WORDS WITH POWER

Peace	Potent	Bright	Beautiful
Joy	Commanding	Clear	Complete
Bliss	Strength	Radiant	Wonderful
Love	Solid	Brimming	Happy
Strong	Grounded	Focused	Faith
unshakable	Unbreakable	Unlimited	Outstanding
Compassion	Firm	Remarkable	Confident
Abundant	Bountiful	Enough	Plenty

EMOTURBO

The EmoTurbo

CHAPTER | 57

When Muhammad Ali went to Africa to fight George Foreman for the heavyweight boxing World Championship, it was widely believed that Ali would be badly beaten. In fact, Foreman's power was so formidable that members of the media, other boxers, and even Ali's own trainers were concerned that Muhammad would be seriously injured or permanently disabled in the bout. Most felt his only chance to survive the fight was to keep moving and try to wear the bigger and stronger Foreman out.

The mood in Ali's ready room just before the fight was funereal. Ali would have none of it. Suddenly he called out to everyone in the room, "What am I going to do?" They answered in unison, "You're gonna dance!" From the dressing room to their entrance into the arena, Ali would shout the question and the chorus would answer. Ali did wear Forman down but it wasn't from dancing. Instead, the "greatest fighter of all time" surprised everyone by lying back on the ropes, covering up, and *taunting George Foreman into a rage.* In the eighth round, when Foreman had literally thrown every punch he had and exhausted his energy, Ali popped off the ropes and sent him to the canvas.

This stunning defeat was brought to you courtesy of the EmoTurbo. The EmoTurbo is not an Italian racing car. It is an internal turbocharger that comes on line when you are meeting an important challenge. The EmoTurbo supplies you with the emotional power you need to do the job. The problem is that most people have an On/Off switch on their EmoTurbo, when they need a throttle.

Emotions transform from obstacles to assets when you can ramp them up or throttle them back as needed.

Here is a powerful process for getting a handle on your EmoTurbo.

POWER BALL

Start by thinking about your upcoming goal or challenge and determine which emotional resources you need to face it. Now use the Field Training Exercise (Chapter 30) to bring up the sensation of energy in between your hands. Once you have the feeling of energy flowing back and forth between your palms, see if you can compress it into a tight ball about the size of a baseball. Once you have compressed the energy into a tight ball, move your palms apart and let the force expand back out to a ball the size of a volleyball. Keep compressing and expanding the force until your energy ball feels tangible. Once you have the feeling, let the ball "sit" on your hands.

Imagine that you are sending the powerful or peaceful emotions you need to meet your challenge down your arm and into the ball. Feel the ball pulse with passionate energy, or sense it radiating calm, but pump the ball full of feeling. Now expand this sphere until it is about the size of a very large beach ball, and continue filling it with emotional energy. Once your energy ball is packed with the desired emotion, move the ball toward your body and pull the energy inside you. Feel the emotions amplifying within your body and simultaneously think about your goals and challenges.

After a few moments, reverse the process; this time create a new ball and imagine all the unwanted feelings and negative emotions being pulled *out* of your body and sucked *into* the ball. Imagine that the fear, anger, or doubt is trapped inside the energy field. Now reduce the ball to the size of a pea and let it go.

Finish the exercise by creating one more power ball. Again, fill it with the desired emotion and pull that energy within you. When you are ready, simply exit the process by opening your eyes. Practice often, experience the power, and integrate the exercise into your warm-up routine, and you will step into the ring feeling like a World Champion.

The Amoeba Syndrome

CHAPTER | 58

When Carolyn Kelly heard the splash, she didn't hesitate to dive in and help, literally. A car with an eighty-three-year-old passenger had rolled away from a nursing home and plunged into a pond. Kelly dove in and held the woman's head above water until help arrived. Carolyn Kelly is eighty-one years old. When asked why she did it, Kelly replied, "There wasn't anybody else around." Taxi driver Rodney Venice didn't have to step in when he saw a man pistol-whipping a woman in a Missouri parking lot, but he did. Grappling with the gunman long enough to allow the woman to drive to safety, Venice was shot three times and died.

Stories like these fly in the face of modern thinking that pain and pleasure is our greatest motivator. When people risk, or give, their lives to save total strangers, it suggests that human beings may have a motivational strategy that is slightly more complex than that of an amoeba. The same holds true for mountain climbers who risk their lives to summit a peak and elite athletes everywhere who sacrifice social life and endure physical hardship to realize a personal record. You are much more than a collection of defense mechanisms out to have a good time.

Contrary to what motivational speakers tell you about avoidance and reward behaviors, the forces that drive you are far more complex and magnificent. Pandering to society's pain phobia, these speakers proselytize that every day can be bliss. Worse, they perpetuate the myth that negative emotions are bad, and if you have them you must be somehow defective or deficient. Great! Now you can be unhappy *and* ashamed about your unhappiness at the same time.

Would you really want to be upbeat and joyful at the funeral of a good friend?

Grief is not a four-letter word, it is a natural process. Suffering is part of life. This is not an easy concept to accept. But anyone who tells you that every day can be "a bowl of cherries" is selling something. *Fortunately, the conflict caused by your problems and the efforts you make to resolve them raises your level of consciousness and causes you to grow.* Managing emotional energy gets much easier when you stop acting like a single-celled organism and learn to trust and use *all* your emotions. Fear causes the rock climber to double check his equipment. Anxiety gives the student the energy to study for a big test. Doubt helps you discover the flaws in your strategy.

Fritz Perls, the fiery gnome of Gestalt Therapy, once said that America made a shift from the "shouldism" of the 1950's to the "hedonism" of the late 60's. Dr. Perls did not see this as a step forward. Perhaps it is time to stop grasping for pleasure and running from pain and, instead, step up to the plate as adults, accepting both our weaknesses and our strengths and acknowledging the value of our suffering. While indulging in painful feelings is a waste of energy, denying them derails Information Transduction and builds a roadblock to personal mastery and growth.

Action Management

Do It Now

CHAPTER | 59

In 1886, David McConnell was a door-to-door book salesman who specialized in the works of William Shakespeare. Since McConnell's target market was "the lady of the house," he offered a bottle of perfume as an incentive to purchase a complete set of books. Unfortunately, no one wanted the books. However, everyone *did* want the perfume, and McConnell was quick enough to notice.

Putting Shakespeare on the shelf, McConnell began selling perfumes and hair care and beauty products. The idea caught on, and McConnell's door-to-door route is the now the largest direct-selling company in the world, with over 6 billion dollars in annual sales. In a tribute to Shakespeare, he named his company after the playwright's place of birth. He called the company Avon.

Information Transduction initiates action. In fact, once IT has built up sufficient energy, it becomes difficult or impossible *not* to take action. Here-and-now attention, an active imagination, and precise communication gives you life strategies that are based on assets and possibility and resonate with reality. The tools of Information Management remove mental tension and push procrastination aside. When you combine them with the skills of Energy Management, you accelerate this movement toward action by eliminating friction from your nervous system. When all the lights are green throughout the mind and body, action becomes inevitable.

However, Avon didn't come into being just because David McConnell had a few good IT skills. Avon was born because McConnell knew the power of *doing it now.*

Moments of penetrating insight and heady revelation fade fast once the imagination loses interest, and the *imagination is only interested in the things that are happening right now.* Search for more information, pencil things out, interview others, but do it now. Think in the present tense. Plan the future by imagining that you are facing the situation today. Present your mind with immediate challenges and *think in terms of the next five steps you need to take.* Tie a deadline to each one and start to work on them right now. Take whatever action you can. No step is too small. Even when you are in doubt, do something. No matter how you feel, do something.

Action in the present activates the neural pathways that deal with your goals and dreams and adds momentum to the IT process. Since Information Transduction leads back to action, energy begins to spiral up and *into* control. Why not create a vicious cycle that works *for* you?

The 180

CHAPTER | 60

Organic chemistry is a dirty business. Tarry residues constantly foul up instruments and equipment and cannot be removed. In 1909, Leo Baekeland decided to clean up organic chemistry's act and invent a solvent that would dissolve this equipment-killing waste. Baekeland whipped up a fresh batch of the tar and started searching for a solvent. The residue was resilient and defeated Leo. He could not find a single substance that would work. That is when the Mr. Clean of organic chemistry put the 180 Principle to work.

It suddenly dawned on Baekeland that if this nearly indestructible substance was resistant to solvents, heat, and water and could be manufactured from "waste," it might have a useful application in its own right. Reversing his intention, the chemist then went to work refining the resinous mass, making it harder, tougher, and easier to mold and to machine. Baekeland created Bakelite, the first of the thermosetting plastics. From the slag of organic chemistry, the Age of Plastics was born.

The same 180-degree principle that created Tupperware is at your disposal. Baekeland's original plan wasn't working, but instead of slamming his head against the wall of repeated failure or blind obsession, the scientist had the good sense to *manage information by turning it over, around, and upside down.*

Examining the polar opposite side of your intentions, your actions, and your emotional responses will almost always produce insight and value. However, turning your world around takes courage. It is difficult to admit when you have been wrong or that you are beating a dead horse, but if what you're doing isn't producing the results you intend, it is time to take a *look at the action or behavior that is 180 degrees, the exact opposite, of what you normally do.*

The same is true for your point of view and attitude. When your outlook is hampering your outcome, it is time to review your situation in the reverse and see what is in store for you. Tired of being on the backburner in your relationship, but complaining and pouting is getting you nowhere? Stop working so hard on being the perfect couple and go find something that *you* love to do. Aerobics class not taking off the weight? Work weight lifting into your training schedule. Teenager has a habit of tuning out when you talk? Try listening more and shouting less. Unhappy in your job? Consider a career that is the exact opposite of what you currently do.

What should you do with the information you find on the inverse side? First, imagine what would happen if you took those actions or saw this situation in that different light or from that point of view. Then absorb any useful information that comes from this process into your life by changing your behavior or by integrating the emerging concepts into your thinking. Whether you act on these ideas or experiment with the unusual concepts that you find on the opposite side is up to you. Sometimes the gift you find in this world of reverse wisdom is a *restoration of confidence* in the rightness of your current actions or original plan. Either way, the contrasting information you find gives you a point of comparison from which you can make a firm decision.

Just remember, if what you are doing isn't working or it is time for a shift in the game plan, there is a wealth of information waiting for you 180 degrees from where you stand.

THE RULE *of* TRANSFORMATION

*"Ideas accepted into the mind
remain until transformed"*

Five Words to Freedom

CHAPTER | 61

In the early 1940's, Raymond Corsini was a psychologist at Auburn prison in upstate New York. One day a prisoner who was about to be released came by Corsini's office to thank him for all he had done. The prisoner said that, thanks to Corsini, he was a changed man. He had stopped fraternizing with the hard-core inmates and gotten his high school diploma. He had reestablished contact with his family, taken a correspondence course in drafting, and even had job waiting for him on the outside. He felt like a new person and the world looked like a different place to him now; even the air smelled different.

Raymond Corsini couldn't remember ever having seen the man. All the files showed was that they had met briefly, some two years prior when the doctor had given the inmate an IQ test. When Corsini suggested that the man had him confused with someone else, the prisoner said with conviction, "It was you alright, and I will never forget what you said to me which changed my life." Slack jawed, Corsini asked what he had said that made such a resounding difference. The prisoner replied, "You told me I had a high IQ."

How could the five simple words "You have a high IQ" have such a profound effect on a person? Obviously, iron bars and concrete walls weren't the only prison that the inmate at Auburn was trapped in. The inmate was also a prisoner of the Mind's Second Rule. Until he heard Corsini's offhand remark, the convict was locked away in an inner cage built of harsh concepts and disparaging ideas concerning his intellectual capacity. His impressions about poor grades, the cutting criticisms from his family and his teachers, and the experience of being shunned for thinking differently than others, merged together and became *fixed concepts* held in his Deeper Mind. While these concepts were often hidden from his conscious awareness and were as far from reality as the Easter Bunny, they still formed the *navigational precepts* that guided this person's life.

Sure, he liked to read Noble Laureate Sinclair Lewis while his friends were enchanted with the action/adventure stories of Edgar Rice Burroughs. And yes, he enjoyed the symphony and chess while his pals listened to popular tunes and played checkers; but until that day in Ray Corsini's office, all the inmate *knew* was that he was crazy and stupid and that insanity and low intelligence were a bad combination. Five words, *spoken at the right time*, forever changed the prisoner's navigational precepts and set his life on a different course.

What information creates, information can change. However, lasting change and growth can only take place when high-powered information penetrates your inner realm of fixed concepts and *transforms* them. The Second Rule holds the key to reaching this arena of imbedded beliefs and creating a personal revolution.

The Parallels

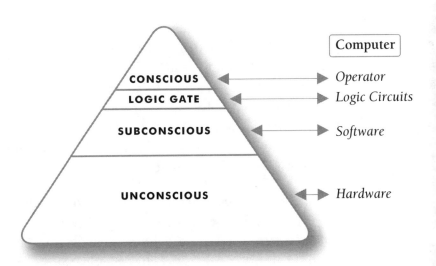

The Boolean Boogie

CHAPTER | 62

From the cradling arms of the forklift to the hand-shaped scoop of a backhoe, humans tend to invent machines that work like they do. Just like the machines that mimic your appendages and movement, today's computer imitates the way your mind operates.

The computer has hardware that includes everything from the mouse, monitor, ports, and cables to the memory and internal systems that give the machine life. You have an Unconscious that comes hardwired into your brain and body and contains your deepest memory banks, core instincts, and life support systems.

The computer has software that, when loaded into the machine, tells the hardware what to do, when to do it, and how to do it. You have a Subconscious, which takes your life experience and converts it into internal programs that tell your brain and body how to *do* almost everything. Hitting a golf ball, making love, facing adversity, and finding a life partner are just a few of the software programs your Subconscious has created over time.

The computer has a series of logic chips that perform problem-solving functions in terms of true or false, and monitor the flow of information. Your internal analyzer and information manager is a thinking mechanism I call the "Logic Gate." Just like its silicon counterpart, the Logic Gate analyzes information and *accepts or rejects that information based on the programs stored in the Subconscious.*

Lastly, the computer has an operator. This is the human being who sits at the keyboard or mouse and gives the computer direction. The operator doesn't have to know Boolean algebra, but she must be able to communicate with the computer in order to get it to function properly. Without the right commands she can bang away at the keyboard until her fingers are numb, but the tiny gnomes inside of the machine will never give her what she wants. Your operator is called the Conscious Mind. Your Conscious Mind doesn't have to study neurosurgery to direct your brain and body, but it does need to be able to communicate with the unseen systems inside of you.

Error messages from the Deeper Mind can be severe. Internal error messages pop up in the form of midlife crises, panic attacks, angry moods, poor performance, or a bad case of the blues. The secret to avoiding these messages lies in Information Management. However, this time, the information is on the inside. To put the Second Rule to use, you must be able to add, delete, or upgrade the software of the Subconscious Mind. When the hardware, software, and problem-solving circuits of the computer meet a competent operator, an amazing amount can be accomplished. When the Conscious Mind begins directing your Subconscious functions, "light-bulb moments" last a lifetime and accelerated learning becomes second nature.

The Rule of Transformation is presented in two sections. Section one explores the three most accessible regions of the mind: the Conscious, the Logic Gate, and the Subconscious. Section two, "The Inner Life," takes on the vast region of the Unconscious and outlines a way to build a powerful relationship with the deepest aspect of your being. The Rule of Transformation will give you a map of the mind, and its exercises will guide you into the territory. If you have the desire to transcend a limitation and the courage to create an internal revolution, then turn the page.

The Subconscious

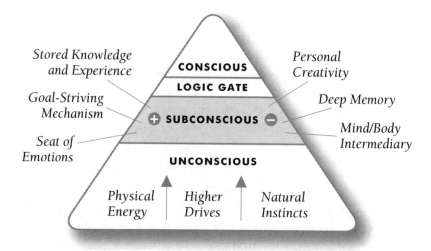

Act Your Age

CHAPTER | 63

What do you get your father for his ninety-ninth birthday? Well, if you are Yuichiro Miura, the first person to ski down Mount Everest, you give dad a ski trip to an avalanche-prone glacier in the French Alps. Dropped off by cable car at 12,700 feet, Keizo Miura braved howling winds and freezing temperatures to ski the famed White Valley with his son and grandson. "What more could I imagine than the Valle Blanche!" Keizo said before skiing down the mountainside.

Eighty-two-year-old Ted Byram of Fort Pierce, Florida, went bowling seventeen days after having a partial stroke. Byram not only bowled, he rolled a perfect game.

At seventy-two, Madonna Buder was the oldest woman competing in the grueling Ironman Triathlon in Hawaii. The retired Catholic nun has raced the 2.4-mile open ocean swim, 112-mile bicycle ride, and 26.2-mile marathon since 1985, finishing fourteen of her sixteen attempts.

Then there is Genshin Fujinami. At forty-four, Fujinami is a Tendai Buddhist monk who has just completed an ancient running ritual in the remote mountains of Japan. Hoping for a shot at enlightenment in this lifetime, Genshin ran 24,800 miles in nothing more than a white robe and flimsy straw sandals. To complete his journey in the required time, Genshin had to run the equivalent of *two Olympic marathons (52.5 miles) every day for 100 days in a row.*

In a youth-obsessed world, the belief about being sidelined by old age is widespread. Somehow Madonna, Ted, Genshin, and Keizo got a different message.

Information that comes from life experience and gets locked into the mind generates powerful *expectations*. Touch a hot stove once or twice and you come to expect that "hot" will burn you. Fall down and the effects of gravity become a given. Along with the hard-and-fast knowledge that comes through interfacing with physical laws, *fixed ideas* on topics like aging, selecting the perfect mate, parenting, and personal capacity also start with personal experience. Interactions with the elderly, the kid who broke your heart in the seventh grade, and your encounters with authority figures were all conscious experiences that drifted from awareness and became the subconscious systems that govern your choices and determine your actions every day. While the memory of falling from the bicycle faded, the expectation that it created remains. See for yourself.

Right now imagine a plank of hardwood lying on level ground. The plank is 4 inches thick, 36 inches wide, and 10 feet long. Now imagine that someone is willing to pay you $1,000 to walk that plank from end to end. Most likely you would grab the money and dance down the board. Next imagine that the offer is the same but now the plank is suspended 500 feet in the air. Chances are you won't be doing the Watusi this time. When the plank hanging in the air is just as wide, sturdy, and safe as when it is resting on solid ground, it is the *expectation of falling*, not the height, that triggers Transduction and creates the fear.

Real or imagined, fixed ideas and the entrenched expectations they produce are impacting you even as you read this sentence.

> *How old would you be*
> *if you didn't know how old you was?*
> −SATCHEL PAIGE−

King Midas In Reverse

CHAPTER | 64

In 1966, Paul Simon turned an Edwin Robinson poem into a popular song. Simon's piece retold the story of Richard Corey, "a banker's only child" who "had everything a man could want: power, grace, and style." Or as Robinson put it, Richard Corey "fluttered pulses" when he talked and "glittered when he walked." The speaker in the poem and the singer in the song both "curse the life I am living" and "curse my poverty" and both very much "wish that I could be Richard Corey." So it is understandable that both narrators are flabbergasted when "the evening headlines read, Richard Corey went home last night and put a bullet through his head."

It is perplexing to all of us when people who seem to have "everything" self-destruct. Elvis ran afoul with gluttony and painkillers. Marilyn couldn't find love even though she had millions of fans. Kurt Cobain silenced his own voice out of self-hatred. How is it that people who have it all can still feel so weak, powerless, and small? The answers lie in the Second Rule of the Mind.

Ideas that are accepted into the mind are stored as *feelings*. This practice of encoding experience as emotions just makes good evolutionary sense. When it comes to survival, time is a critical element. Thinking consumes valuable time, while feelings move you to action much faster. As one martial arts teacher put it, "If you have to think about a punch coming toward you, it is already too late." As information becomes streamlined and sinks into the Subconscious, the what-happened memories fade but the how-it-felt memories remain. Working like a computer, the mind handles issues of storage and operating speed by compressing information into an emotion or a series of feelings. Important information is charged with emotional energy for quick retrieval and linked to other concepts that have common elements or that share similar feelings.

Marilyn, Elvis, and Kurt were working with some very bad information and accepted some seriously life-negating ideas (Chapter 14) into their minds. Over time, these anti-life messages evolved into *predetermined* feelings of hopelessness, helplessness, or loathing. With their expectations and emotions preset, even the adoring faces of their fans could trigger feelings of loneliness and isolation. All three of these superstars knew *intellectually* that they were successful, but that information just wasn't powerful enough to penetrate into the feeling mind and transform the fixed ideas, expectations, and emotions locked in there. Like the inmate from Auburn Prison, Marilyn, Elvis, and Kurt needed a blockbuster of an idea to enter the mind at exactly the right time.

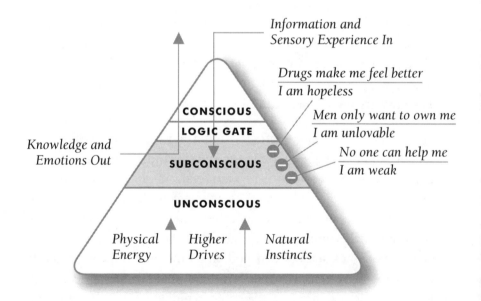

The Kansas Flyer

CHAPTER | 65

The fire in the school had taken the life of his brother, and now the doctors were saying that his burns were going to cost him both his legs. Besides, they said, even if the legs could be saved he would never walk again. The seven-year-old burn victim told the physicians that, not only would he keep his legs and walk, *one day he would run faster than any man on earth.*

The road to recovery was long and filled with excruciating pain, but Glenn Cunningham endured. Ten years after the tragedy, Cunningham joined the Elkhart High School Track Team. By 1936 "The Kansas Flyer" had advanced to the Olympics, winning the silver medal in the 1500 meters in Berlin. In 1938, Glenn Cunningham lived up to his word and became the fastest man on earth by running the mile in 4:04.4. When his running career ended, the boy who refused to give up his legs owned *twelve of the thirty-one fastest times on record.*

Children live almost exclusively on the Subconscious side of the mind. Until the thinking centers of the brain develop, kids are information sponges, absorbing ideas into the Subconscious almost effortlessly. This *uncritical acceptance* of incoming information gives children an advantage in learning language, acquiring a new skill, or tapping their creative energy. In addition to a natural tendency to soak up information, Glenn Cunningham's young mind was laid open by trauma. Unlike the prisoner from Auburn Penitentiary, whose fixed ideas took shape over time and through the *repetition* of negative experience and harsh criticism, the vows that Cunningham made to the doctors on that day rocketed directly into his

Subconscious and immediately took over as the primary precepts guiding his life. Like the scars that would form on his legs, the idea of being the world's fastest man was permanently burned into Glenn Cunningham's mind.

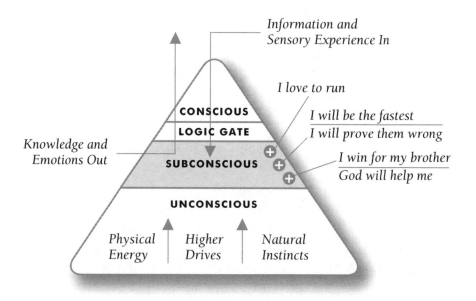

Fixed ideas can make your life a prison but they also hold the power to set you free. Life-negating or life-affirming, *any idea that is accepted by the mind remains until it is replaced or transformed by another idea.* When your dreams become important to the Subconscious, they tap all the passion and determination that the feeling mind has to offer. In addition to this driving motivation, your goals gain unlimited access to the Deeper Mind's most important resource, creativity.

Life-affirming ideas that make their way into the Subconscious build expectations just like their negative counterparts. The inward expectation of eventual success puts millionaires back on their feet after they have lost it all, and helps competitors stage a comeback when everyone else has written them off. Positive mental expectation also paves the way for super Transduction as your brain and body literally become *conditioned to win* (Chapter 37). Your dreams do not have to be forged in a dramatic trial by fire like Glenn Cunningham's, but they must reach and arouse your feeling mind.

The Dueling Pool

C H A P T E R | 66

In a classic Indian story, a novice monk and his teacher are walking together when they come to a river. On the river bank they meet a young woman who asks if one of the monks could carry her across since there is no bridge. The novice monk, thinking that touching her might not be very monk-like behavior, refuses. His teacher, however, quickly picks up the woman and fords the waterway. Reaching the other side, the teacher sets her down, and he and the novice resume their journey.

As they walk, the younger monk keeps thinking about the incident at the river. It troubles him. Perhaps his teacher has made a mistake. Mile after mile the novice monk inwardly debates the ethics of such conduct. Finally, when he can't take it anymore, he turns to the teacher and asks, "Do you think it was right for you to pick up that woman and carry her?" The teacher smiles and replies, "I put her down after we crossed the river. You are still carrying her."

Opposing ideas that become fixed in the mind create conflict throughout the nervous system. The singer who accepts the fact that she has a gifted voice, but also believes that it is somehow boastful to display her talent, is likely to have a very short career. The father who demands total honesty from his children, but who rationalizes cheating on his spouse, will experience physical stress. The dieter who *talks* about eating right and exercising regularly, but whose concepts of physical comfort and gratification prevent her from ever taking action, is heading for the pit of low self-esteem.

Fixed ideas that are in opposition create tension, procrastination, indecision, and indifference. Like dueling pools of energy in the brain, ideas that are in conflict cancel each other out and sap vital ego strength. However, replace just one of the opposing ideas with a more *cooperative* point of view and a chain reaction in the mind and body begins.

When Subconscious opposition is converted to agreement, the energy that was bound up in resistance is released physically and emotionally. This rush of insight and release of pent-up power is the reason people faint, become excited, weep, or laugh in the middle of a light-bulb moment. It is the force that makes you say, "Aha!" When this wave of energy hits the nervous system, you jump the fixed neural tracks in your brain and establish new pathways. If these new pathways are reinforced through action and nurtured by attention and information, they become fixed and remain in the mind until a concept with higher voltage comes along and causes them to change.

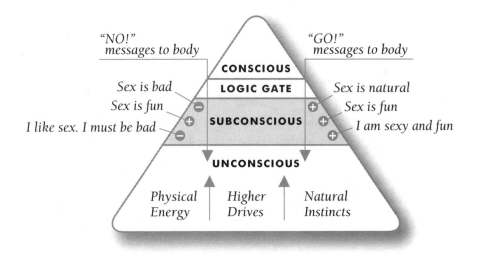

Replace a single fixed idea and it will send a powerful ripple though your inner world. Remove the opposition in your mind and you will start a revolution.

A Final Word On Fixed Ideas

CHAPTER | 67

You probably don't remember the first time you were burned and you probably will never forget the first time you had sex but, consciously remembered or not, major life events like these have made a deep impression in your Subconscious Mind. Hopefully, both these experiences were appropriately "hot."

From the time you were born to the present day, you have been collecting ideas and your Subconscious has been weaving these disparate threads into a common tapestry. Conflicting and cooperative programs are tied together, and fact and fantasy have been woven side by side.

Just as tapestries were the first newspapers, the story of your life is written in the headlines of your Subconscious. These patterns of interconnected and fixed ideas have become your philosophy about your past, your future, and your place in this world. The conclusions you have come to, and the expectations you hold, create the nucleus of your personality and determine your ability to "play well with others."

In the long run, fixed ideas are simply pools of condensed information that lie dormant in the mind until activated by a signal from one or all of the senses. The fear of public speaking, the defeatist outlook, or the feeling of being unlovable—all the embarrassment, helplessness, or pain they produce are no more than internalized ideas that are subject to *change*. Change one thread in a tapestry and you alter the entire picture. Change one fixed idea that you hold in your Subconscious and you alter your future. But to reach this Deeper Mind, you will have to get past the Logic Gate.

> *As in Rome there is, apart from the Romans,*
> *a population of statues, so apart from this real world*
> *there is a world of illusion, almost more potent,*
> *in which most men live.*
>
> —GOETHE—

The Logic Gate

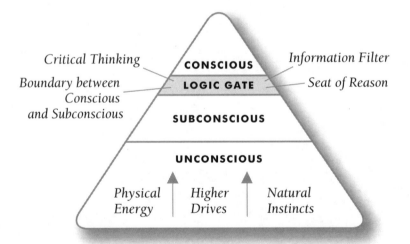

The Logic Gate

CHAPTER | 68

In the original *Star Trek* television show, James T. Kirk is captain of a starship that travels the galaxy seeking out new life on distant planets. Kirk is a fiery, heroic leader whose curious nature and passion often get him and his crew into do-or-die situations. When that happens, the burden of coming up with a solution falls on the ship's first officer, Mr. Spock. Spock is from the planet Vulcan. His ancestors determined that emotions were problematic and that the function of logic should predominate in the mind. Banishing their feelings to some distant sector of their brain, they became disciples of reason. So when Kirk's bravado gets the ship into dire straits, Spock uses reasoning and analysis to come up with a solution to save the captain's bacon.

The relationship between your internal reasoning center and your Subconscious Mind bears a sharp resemblance to the interactions between Captain Kirk and Mr. Spock.

Kirk's bias for emotional decision making, his driving need to explore, and his inclination for romancing aliens put him squarely on the side of the Feeling Mind. Spock, with his preference for reason and logic, represents the analytical Thinking Mind. Time and time again, the Feeling Mind starts something that the Thinking Mind must find a way to accomplish or resolve. A sudden infatuation with a coworker, the impulse to take flying lessons, or that super-heated argument you had with your brother — all become porcupines that land in the lap of the Thinking Mind.

When you were born, you were mostly "Kirk." You made moral judgments and based your decisions entirely on your feelings.

Somewhere in middle childhood, you began to develop more of your "Spock" side. You matured as your mind built the Logic Gate. Today, the Logic Gate gives you the ability to reason and to get things done. Without a Logic Gate, you would have all the desire to achieve your goals but your only tool to attain them would be your instincts. Without the aid of critical thinking, you would be incapable of developing an effective action plan.

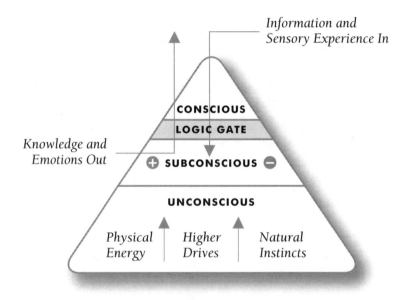

The Logic Gate is also the boundary line between the Conscious and the Subconscious, and forms your threshold of awareness. This inner buffer protects you from being overwhelmed by your feelings and, when working properly, stops you from responding to irrational ideas such as the bogeyman. Like its computer chip counterpart, the Logic Gate processes information but *does not store it*. Information on the Conscious side of the Gate is visible to you, but once that same information slips through the boundary and into the Deeper Mind, it becomes hidden from your view.

With one foot on either side, the Gate also controls *access* to the Subconscious and grants or denies the passage of information into or out of the mind. Comparing the information coming into your conscious awareness with the fixed ideas held in the Subconscious, the Logic Gate quickly accepts data that is congruent and already known to the Deeper Mind. Information that is incompatible and unknown to the Subconscious is suspended, further analyzed, or *flatly rejected*. Few experiences are more frustrating that being consciously aware of a problem or seeing its solution, but being unable to get these new ideas to stick in the mind because the Logic Gate is locked. Fear not. Your inner Kirk and Spock can work together and save the galaxy every time.

A Brief History of Inhibition

CHAPTER | 69

Comedian W. C. Fields ran away from home when he was eleven years old. His one-of-a-kind voice came from continuous exposure to bitter cold and his trademark red nose from fighting with older kids on the street. By twenty-one he was a vaudeville headliner, and by forty-five he was an internationally acclaimed movie star. He wrote the films that he starred in and the characters he portrayed were always men of many vices. One vice that Fields shared with his on-screen alter egos was an adoration of alcoholic beverages. Martinis were a staple on the movie sets where he worked, and a drink was never far off when he wrote. W. C. Fields felt that gin *released* his comedic genius.

Using drugs or alcohol to access the Feeling Mind and generate creativity is nothing new. Lewis Carroll, John Lennon, Dylan Thomas, and countless others penned a good line or two when they were pie-eyed. Even Winston Churchill spoke about champagne as if it were inspiration served in a glass. Since the Greeks, people have drunk to relax, drunk to forget, drunk to ratchet up their courage, or drunk to loosen up and dance. Why this ancient love affair with alcohol? When the Logic Gate gets overloaded, it slams shut. Alcohol is a battering ram that knocks the Gate off its hinges.

Critical thinking takes time and requires energy, so when the pressure is on to produce, information entering your logic centers can back up quickly. In addition, your brain and body are primed to feel first and reason later. This means that the Logic Gate must handle both the onslaught of information coming into the Conscious Mind, as well as the emotional pressure welling up from the Subconscious. To maintain control in the middle of this double whammy, the Logic Gate inhibits the rate at which information is converted into energy and back again. Tension mounts, conflicting fixed ideas do battle, and you feel this internal friction as frustration and irritation. Finally, unable to cope with the information and energy flow, the critical thinking part of the mind hits critical mass and, usually, becomes hypercritical of itself. The Thinking Mind locks down and you lock up.

Writers' block, a pitching slump, or poor sexual performance are all examples of this bottleneck in the brain. Overloaded with information and overwhelmed by emotion, the Logic Gate collapses and the Feeling Mind steps forward to run the show. Depending on the fixed ideas held at the Subconscious level, this internal shift can be the road to heaven or the highway to hell. But before you turn to booze in an effort to do an end run around the Logic Gate, please remember, intoxicants can't give you anything that isn't already inside. Your power on the speakers' podium, comfort in the bedroom, or performance on the field, all *do* increase when your inhibition goes offline, but that response is best brought on by training the nervous system and learning to trust your Subconscious side. Your success lies in working with the Thinking Mind, not rendering it comatose.

The good news is that you have already begun teaching the Thinking Mind how and when to step aside. Every time you set aside judgment in the Field Training Exercise (Chapter 30), bypass thinking and tune into your senses with E.S.P. (Chapter 18), or take a trip to the Imagymnasium (Chapters 51, 52), you forge a relationship with your deeper nature. Intentionally turning over control to your Subconscious allows your Logic Gate to rest, regroup, and grow stronger. A strong Gate helps you to stay focused and to function at your fullest every day.

> *All I can say is that I have taken more out of alcohol*
> *than it has taken out of me.*
> —WINSTON CHURCHILL—

Overload

The room was one hundred times darker than the darkest of nights. Standing outside on the porch, I could hear the flames sucking up oxygen and biting into wood. Heat and smoke stormed out the front door like an angry, black wind. The house was on fire and, in a moment, I was about to walk through that same door and go inside.

In what seems like another life, I was a park ranger at a lake on the sunny central coast of California. I spent most of the 1980's as part of a team that provided law enforcement, emergency medical assistance, and fire suppression to thousands of recreational enthusiasts. That is how I ended up in a burning building. The plan was simple. A team of trainers from the California Department of Forestry (CDF) would set an abandoned farmhouse on fire and the rangers would takes turns going inside and putting it out. We would get some exposure to fighting a structure fire and the farmer would get rid of an eyesore on his property.

Waiting at the door for the signal to enter the building, I was working hard to override some fixed ideas I had about BURNING TO DEATH and fighting my body's wise desire to RUN when one of the trainers dropped a bomb on my Subconscious. Just as the word was given for my team to "GO!", one of the CDF trainers began screaming in a pleading falsetto, "Save my baby! My baby is in there! Save my baby!" Now, I *knew* that there was no baby in there, and his impression of a desperate mother was pretty weak. Nevertheless, in the heat of the moment, that additional piece of information blew out my Logic Gate and the suggestion that a child was in danger exploded in my Feeling

Mind. Against all rational understanding, and with a huge rush of energy, I plunged into the smoke-filled room like Batman.

Anytime the Logic Gate swings open, your Subconscious becomes accessible to you. Just as strong feelings can flood up from the Deeper Mind, *unscreened information can pour into the Subconscious*. The mother who hits the end of her rope and screams at her children has to deal with new information about being a "bad" mommy. Cracking under pressure at a crucial moment in a tournament may cause a player to wrestle with his worth as a person later on. On the other hand, discovering a hidden talent or finding a new resource when you are in the heat of battle can galvanize your resolve and bring newfound power and hope.

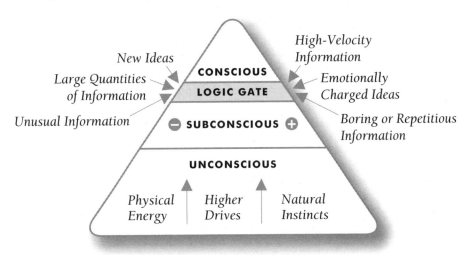

Essentially, this process of moving the Logic Gate aside and making an impression in the Deeper Mind is the same one used by hypnotists to help their clients change and grow. Instead of a burning building, the hypnotist uses new ideas, unique images, and unusual experiences to *overload* the client's Logic Gate and get a message across to the Subconscious Mind.

Another tool the hypnotist uses to unlock the Logic Gate is *fatigue*. Words like "sleep, rest, and relaxation" have no content that can be processed logically. Repeated monotonously, these concepts bore the Logic Gate, and it responds by moving toward sleep. Without the interference of overanalysis by your logical partner, the ideas given to you when you are near sleep often reach the Deeper Mind intact and take hold.

You will have mastered the Rule of Transformation when you can intentionally open this inner door and change the fixed ideas you hold inside. No fire engines or swinging pocket watches are required.

During periods of great stress, words that seem immaterial or are uttered in jest might become fixed in the patient's mind and cause untold harm. This means being extremely careful about what is said at the scene [of an accident].
—ACADEMY OF ORTHOPEDIC SURGEONS—

What Were They Thinking

CHAPTER | 71

Tonya Harding was a contender in the 1994 Olympic figure skating competition. One big obstacle stood between Tonya and all the lucrative commercial opportunities that come with winning a Gold Medal—her teammate Nancy Kerrigan. Hoping to clear Tonya's way to the winner's podium, Harding's live-in ex-husband, Jeff Gillooly, hatched a not-so-elaborate plot to take Nancy out of the competition. During the 1994 National Championships, Gillooly hired a thug named Shane Stant to wait outside the practice rink and whack Kerrigan in the knee with a baton as she was leaving.

From having a motive to making a series of incriminating phone calls, all the evidence pointed immediately to Harding and Gillooly. In fact, the evidence was so direct and obvious that it left news reporters incredulously asking, "What were they thinking?" The short answer is, "They weren't." For all the planning that likely went into this scheme, thinking was not part of the process. In the end, bruised but not broken, Nancy Kerrigan came back with a vengeance and took the Silver Medal in Lillehammer. Tonya, who denied knowledge of the plan, skated but did not make it to the podium. Gillooly and Stant were arrested.

Strong feelings such as pride, greed, jealousy, fear, or even love overwhelm the Thinking Mind.

Gripped by fear or greed, people become highly motivated *but lose the asset of critical thinking*. That is why greed, fear, and pride are the devices of con men, unscrupulous salesmen, and bad politicians everywhere. Adolph Hitler used these very tools to start World War II. Personal reward, fear of the Jews, and pride in the Fatherland became the smokescreens that clouded the reasoning of an entire nation. Once heady emotions like these are stirred, the Logic Gate produces little more than propaganda in the form of rationalization and justification of the desires rising up from the Feeling Mind. Of course, after the spell fades and the misdeeds or atrocities have been committed, the Logic Gate returns to a more objective position. Now the ramifications and true motivations for our actions become clear, and healthy people experience regret.

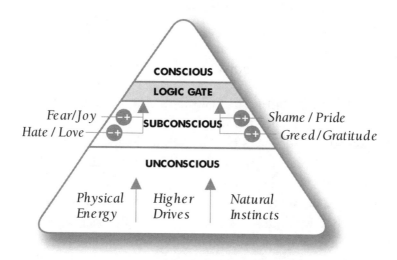

The power of the Feeling Mind to take over, once the Thinking Mind is overwhelmed, explains why your cousin Bob left his wonderful family for an overweight bimbo with bad teeth. It accounts for that feeling of buyer's remorse that often follows major purchases that were wanted far more than they were needed. It is the reason that even good people can do some very wrong things.

How can you avoid making the costly decisions brought on by emotional logic? Start by using your emotions as a signpost. *Whenever strong emotions are prompting your decisions, make it a point to slow down your rate of transduction and consult the Thinking Mind.* First, manage your energy: Breathe, relax, or tune into your senses (E.S.P.) but get out of your IT meltdown. Then, manage the information more effectively by using the Logic Gate and giving the issue a thorough critical review. This simple act helps build ego strength and just may keep you out of trouble.

The Conscious

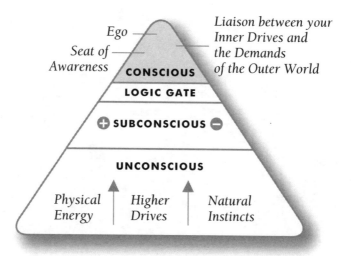

Ego

Seat of
Awareness

Liaison between your
Inner Drives and
the Demands
of the Outer World

CONSCIOUS

LOGIC GATE

➕ **SUBCONSCIOUS** ➖

UNCONSCIOUS

Physical   Higher   Natural
Energy   Drives   Instincts

Eros, Logos Ego

CHAPTER | 72

Nasrudin is a cross between a saint and a wise guy. Tales of this mythic, holy man/fool have circled the globe because every spoonful of wisdom they contain is accompanied by a smile. In one story, Nasrudin is given a check and goes down to the bank to cash it. The bank teller quickly approves the check but casts a doubtful eye on the disheveled mullah saying, "Your check looks fine, Mr. Nasrudin, but can you identify yourself?" "Of course," replies the holy man. Taking a mirror out of his pocket, Nasrudin looks at his reflection and sighs, "Yes, that is me."

You are conscious of your world because you can see, hear, smell, taste, and feel it. However, while these sense perceptions can tell you that something *is*, they can not tell *what* it is. To fully understand the nature of an object or an event, your Conscious Mind employs a process known as *apperception*. Nasrudin used apperception to identify himself in the bank.

The image in the looking glass was nothing more than reflected light until Nasrudin *compared* what he was seeing with all the memory-images of faces stored in his Subconscious. Comparison and differentiation, with some assistance from his memory, allowed Nasrudin to recognize his face in the mirror. To discriminate this from that, mine from yours, and up from down, the Conscious uses the Thinking Mind to process information. However, apperception doesn't stop there. While thinking can tell you what something is, you need *feeling* to tell you what it is worth, whether it is pleasant or unpleasant, or if it is right or wrong. Once the item or issue is identified, the Conscious begins to *evaluate* the information with the Feeling Mind. Your conclusions are now assessed in terms of how you feel about them. In other words, as our friend Nasrudin recognizes the information in the mirror as his face, he then evaluates that information in feeling terms like, "Wow, I look good!" or "God, I look fat!" As comparison and evaluation combine, *desire* is born. So after recognizing his image and evaluating its condition Nasrudin decides, "I want to get my beard trimmed," or "I want to lose weight."

If this process of comparison and evaluation is conscious and directed, then desire becomes *planning*, and the information is sent back to the Thinking Mind for further processing. If the apperception process is out of your awareness and undirected, it becomes *fantasy* and floats around in the Feeling Mind. If Nasrudin switches to planning mode, he may make an appointment with the barber. If he does nothing to direct the process, his desire to lose weight becomes an internal movie of finally fitting into that little black robe or fighting crime as a buffed superhero.

Comparison and evaluation are tools. Unfortunately, for far too many people, the tools have taken over. For them, *everything* must be associated with a fixed idea from the past and judged by a current set of likes or dislikes in order to make sense. Unnecessary and unfair comparison is a trap, and the critical evaluation it produces is a waste of energy. Moreover, ceaseless apperception saps strength from your important life dreams and can easily send you off to fantasyland. Comparing and evaluating yourself, your situation, or the other individuals in your world does *not* have to be a full-time job.

As you go through this week, pay attention to the way you use the Conscious tools of recognition and evaluation and make an effort to *choose* when you march in the apperception parade.

Stop Trying

A young man travels across Asia to the school of a famous martial artist. At the dojo doorstep he is stopped by the master who asks, "What do you wish from me?"

"I wish to be your student and become the greatest martial artist in the world," the young man replies, "How long must I study?"

"Ten years," the master answers.

"Ten years! That is a long time. What if I study harder than all your other students?" the young man inquires.

"Twenty years," replies the master.

"Twenty years! What if I practice day and night?"

"Thirty years," the master answers.

Exasperated the young man stammers, "How is it that each time I say I will try harder, you tell me that it will take longer?"

Calmly the master replies, "The answer is simple. When one eye is fixed upon your destination, there is only one eye left with which to find the Way."

While the Conscious Mind likes to think it is the boss, it is actually more of a glorified errand boy. Home to your ego, the Conscious mediates between your external reality and the ideas, emotions, and drives that emanate from the Deeper Mind and the physical body. From getting breakfast to finding a soul mate, the Conscious has a full-time job meeting the demands of life *and* satisfying the needs and goals of the Subconscious. Sometimes it seems as if the Subconscious isn't cooperating. When that happens, the Conscious Mind has to flex its muscle in the form of willpower. When the "I am" of your ego comes up with an "I want," it is up to "I will" to get things done. However, in a showdown with the Feeling Mind, your Conscious can't even spell w-i-l-l-p-o-w-e-r. The will is then left to command, threaten, and cajole the Subconscious like a parent trying to get a teenage son or daughter to take out the trash. The results are about the same.

Whining, blaming, and hoping will not get you the cooperation you are looking for. Without the buy-in from your Subconscious side, all the will in the world will never be enough. Since you can't send the Subconscious to its room for a time-out, should you just give up on using willpower? Hardly.

Your Conscious Mind needs to become a leader, with vision and a solid plan for realizing your goals. Your ego needs to understand the contribution that a unified mind can make, and must learn to use the tools of thinking and feeling as they were intended. Finally, the ego needs to make your dreams *important* to the Subconscious. To do that, you need to know how to reach and awaken the Deeper Mind.

Thinking with the Whole Mind

In 1961, an interesting article appeared in the *American Journal of Clinical Hypnosis*. Psychologists hypnotized a university instructor known for his mathematical brilliance. The doctors then suggested to the subject that when he was awakened, he would work on a series of calculus problems with a speed and accuracy greater than anything he had accomplished before. The professor was roused from his trance, provided with the problems, and asked to accurately solve as many as possible in twenty minutes. In the next twenty minutes, he accomplished what normally would have taken him a full two hours to do. *The professor increased his already prodigious speed a remarkable sixfold and still maintained his accuracy.*

When asked how he accomplished this mental feat, the teacher explained that he had jumped over steps in the calculus process and performed calculations in his head that he ordinarily would have had to write out on paper. No one was more surprised by the performance than the professor himself. Not only had he increased his speed, but he confessed to the researchers that, while he normally found calculus drudgery, working on the problems this time was actually *fun*.

Few subjects are more misunderstood than hypnosis. However, when you grasp the nature of the relationship between the Conscious and Subconscious, the process that produced this mathematical miracle becomes crystal clear. All hypnosis did was open the professor's Logic Gate and get his Subconscious Mind to *accept* the calculus challenge *uncritically* (Chapter 65). Uncritical acceptance allowed the teacher to function without comparison, past association, or predetermined limitations getting in the way. In the afterglow of hypnosis, the Conscious Mind supplied attention to the math problems and offered a guiding hand, but had the good sense to trust the Subconscious and let it take it from there. Uninhibited, the professor's Subconscious poured the full force of its creativity and intuition into the calculus and got the job done.

The fun the professor described comes from the freedom of working with the unrestricted energy of the Feeling Mind. His surprise at his own production is actually typical, whenever the ego peers over the Logic Gate and catches a glimpse of the inner workings and power found in the Subconscious Mind. In reality, hypnosis didn't give the professor any extraordinary power; it just helped put his mental house in order.

While this brief inquiry can hardly be called conclusive research, it does point to what is possible when you start to work with a well-coordinated mind. In the boardroom, the bedroom, or on the baseball diamond, any time you are "on your game," the Conscious, Logic Gate, and Subconscious are all working in one direct line. Instead of Conscious domination and willful control, each aspect of the mind is performing its intended function and contributing to the whole.

Creating your own version of the professor's mathematical magic trick simply requires one important thing. You must get the goal-striving, goal-achieving part of your mind to accept a challenge. Once the Subconscious takes up your banner, I promise, the power you find there will astonish you as much as it did the professor.

The Tools of Transformation

The Three Gifts

C H A P T E R | 75

In Sanskrit, the name Siddhartha means "one who has attained his goal." In Hermann Hesse's classic work by the same name, Siddhartha is a spiritual seeker living in India about 2,500 years ago. At one point on his journey toward enlightenment, Siddhartha meets a girl and decides to renounce his austere life as a yogi and get a real job.

When asked by a wealthy merchant during an interview, "What are you able to do?" Siddhartha replied, "I can think. I can wait. I can fast." When the merchant scoffs at the value of these three traits, Siddhartha explains that "If a person has nothing to eat, then fasting is the cleverest thing he can do."

The young sage goes on to say that if he was impatient and driven by hunger, he would be forced to take any job that was offered to him regardless of position or salary, including the one with the merchant. On the other hand, with these inner skills at his disposal, Siddhartha can wait until he finds work that suits him best. The merchant is impressed and Siddhartha gets both the job and the girl.

When Siddhartha says that he can think, wait, and fast, he is describing the role that Consciousness plays in personal growth. Thinking is the ability to put the Logic Gate to good use. Organizing information, making comparisons, evaluating importance, and developing a plan of action all have a place in the creation and fulfillment of your life dreams. "Waiting" refers to the control that the Conscious exerts over the impulsive and emotionally driven nature of the Feeling Mind. The Subconscious has the reasoning ability and emotional maturity of a very bright nine-year-old child.

From laughing at bathroom humor to being shy, selfish, impatient, or nosy, without some Conscious restraint, the Feeling Mind can display all the less-than-charming qualities we see in children. The Conscious must work like a good parent who builds strong self-esteem by defining clear boundaries. "Fasting" is Siddhartha's way of saying, "when life gives you lemons, manage the information in your head and direct the energy in your body." Siddhartha is referring to your Conscious capacity for redirecting your attention to your assets, resources, and choices in time of hardship or adversity (Chapter 14).

Some pain and discomfort on the road to your dreams is to be expected. Life experiences like the loss of an important relationship, poor health, or financial trouble all require the Conscious to become a leader and to rouse the internal resources of the Deeper Mind. If your Conscious Mind won't lead or can't manage hardship and rally, you will not make it through. Fortunately, personal power comes as a byproduct of using the Three Gifts. To meet challenge and rise above adversity, you must learn to cultivate Siddhartha's ability to think, wait, and fast. I suggest you start small.

Thinking starts when you focus your day-to-day attention on your goals and dreams and start asking the right questions. You develop your waiting side by saying "no" when petty moods and emotions rear up from the Subconscious. Listen to others instead of impulsively expounding your opinion or automatically leaping to your own defense. Practice patience when you are waiting in line, particularly if you are pressed for time. Fasting doesn't have to be drastic change in diet — it simply means not being a slave to every whim of the body that happens along. You can instill this important skill by refusing to obey the candy dish at work or exercising when you don't feel like it.

Siddhartha told the merchant that thinking, waiting, and fasting were more precious than gold because, with them, he could accomplish anything. Harness these skills of the Conscious Mind in the insignificant things and you will find the strength you need to make the meaningful ones happen. If ego strength grows in direct proportion to your self-control and can be found even in the small things, why not start now? The next few exercises involve organizing information and putting your Thinking Mind to use; make a commitment to complete them.

Fighting Fire with Water

CHAPTER | 76

Somewhere between 350 and 400 A.D., the Huns made a slight modification to an idea from India which turned their armies into an invincible fighting force. It was one of those inventions that make you slap yourself on the forehead and exclaim, "Now why didn't I think of that?" the instant you see it. The Huns virtually lived on horseback. Their speed and maneuverability in battle was unrivaled, but there was one problem with the mounted warfare of the day: A rider could be unhorsed rather easily. The new weapon that gave the Huns their invincibility was the stirrup.

Invented in India about two centuries prior, the stirrup was originally a leather strap into which a rider could insert his big toe and keep himself balanced when on horseback. The Huns improved on the Indians' idea by making metal stirrups that fit the rider's entire foot. Before the invention of the full-foot stirrup, mounted soldiers could only shoot an arrow or cast a spear. Armed with this updated version, a horseman could *thrust* a spear and put the full weight of the man *and* his horse behind it. Since horses had served as transportation and cavalry for a thousand years before the invention of the stirrup, it makes one wonder what took our ancestors so long to come up with such a simple idea.

My clients express a similar sense of astonishment when new information replaces or transforms the old, fixed ideas they had been carrying around. The instant the concepts that create denial, stubbornness, or self-imposed limitation are transformed, these clients express their surprise in statements like "Why didn't I see this before? It was right there all the time." Or the ever popular, "That's not my stuff!" Interestingly, the concepts that bring on this personal transformation are usually not very complicated or advanced. Just as warfare was revolutionized by something as simple as the stirrup, it is the most elemental ideas that seem to have the biggest impact on the mind.

Whether you use immense ideas culled from the works of the great philosophers or work with the mini-realizations that come from your everyday life, your internal transformation depends on information. In the Rule of Performance, you used information to manage Transduction as it was occurring and affecting your functioning in the outer world. In the Rule of Transformation, your goal is to use information to predetermine your Transduction *before* IT begins. It is time for your Conscious Mind to round up the information you need and put it to work.

Step one is to *organize* the information you want to internalize. If you have not done so already, *pick a challenge, goal, or dream* that you can achieve using this process. Since you are dealing with the goal-striving and goal-achieving aspect of the mind, you must give it something to move toward. Goals are a measuring stick for marking your progress, which is critical when you are dealing with a Thinking Mind that thrives on feedback and a Feeling Mind that is energized by encouragement.

In organizing the information that represents your dreams and deeds, writing plays a big part. The physical act of tracking the words with your eyes, moving your hand to write, or tapping your fingers to type sends a message to your Subconscious via your nervous system. Before you have finished jotting down the first sentence, your Deeper Mind goes to work building the neural highways that will carry your ideas. More important, the process of writing and editing takes *attention and thought*. The very act of organizing your ideas and setting them down to paper focuses the mind, gets the body involved, and stimulates the imagination.

I know that it is tempting to skip this part and just read on, but I urge you to devote some time to organizing and clarifying the dreams in your mind. Here is some incentive. *Every one of my clients who has approached this process seriously and invested their energy in defining their dreams and formulating an action plan has achieved or exceeded their intended goal.* Let's get started.

Think back to the simplicity of the stirrup. Can you *describe* your dream in one sentence? O.K., I'll give you two sentences but no more than fifty words. Come on, find a pen and see how succinct you can get about something you want to be, do, or have.

_____

_____

_____

_____

EXAMPLE

Wrong: "I want to find the cure for cancer, win an Academy Award, never eat chocolate or pizza again, and always be happy."

Right: "To become tobacco free by [date here] and to work out at least three times a week."

Your Finest Hour

CHAPTER | 77

The year was 1940. The dark, evil cloud of the Nazi storm lay across Europe. Since four out of five Americans wanted nothing to do with another world war, the United States was nowhere to be seen. Only the island nation of England stood against the growing German might. Alone, outnumbered, and outgunned, the British faced the wrath of a vengeful and bloodthirsty Adolph Hitler. Nightly bombing raids were killing thousands by the month, and attacks on the English merchant fleet had reduced the diet to about one egg and a few ounces of meat per person per week. That is when Winston Churchill unveiled his most powerful weapon. Churchill hurled *ideas* at the Germans. Or, as reporter Edward R. Murrow said, "[Churchill] mobilized the English language and sent it into battle."

These conceptual salvos were fired off as a series of magnificent speeches broadcast worldwide. Churchill's speeches stirred the souls of his countrymen and softened America's heart. Great Britain responded and took the fight to the Germans while America overcame its isolationist ideology and joined the fray. In the end it was, as Winston had hoped, their "Finest Hour."

Just as Churchill inspired England and transformed America's thinking with nothing more than ideas and language, you must find the concepts and phrases that charge you with energy and create change at your core. To do this you will have to harness the inherent power of information and send a letter to the Subconscious. Written in the language of the Deeper Mind, your letter must be clear, descriptive, and filled with feeling to be effective. Since we are dealing with a mind that operates like a very bright child, it is best to keep your letter brief but exciting. Three paragraphs of potent concepts that fire up the Subconscious are better than three volumes of vague notions that lack emotional luster. However, this letter is more than just a wish list of feel-good affirmations.

In the world of the Subconscious, solid information equals results. Your punchy, three-paragraph dispatch must embody the *ideas that you want to transform into action.* Your letter must contain concise concepts about *what* must happen, *how* it is to be done, and *when* the action will take place or when the task will be completed (Chapter 35). Like the exercises in Intentional Daydreaming (Chapters 26, 27, 28), your letter must cover the mental and physical components of your goal as well as the emotional aspects of your challenge or transformation. Tell yourself, "I love golf!" ten thousand times, but be sure to give the Subconscious the *facts* about the best way to grip the club or how to follow through.

Following are the seven guidelines for speaking the language of the Subconscious Mind. These seven rules apply no matter what your native tongue, and they are quite effective when dealing with the Subconscious side of every other person on the planet. These guidelines will show you how to structure your ideas in a way that the Subconscious understands. Start with the goal statement you made in the last essay and work these seven guidelines into your correspondence with the Deeper Mind. Then prepare yourself to be surprised.

THE 7 GUIDELINES
FOR INFLUENCING THE DEEPER MIND

Make It Personal

When it comes to dealing with the Subconscious, it really is all about you. You can't change anyone else or chose how other people will feel toward you, any more than you can influence the weather on the day of your big tournament or race. Fill your letter with information about the things *you* can control, the attitudes *you* want to adopt, and the actions *you* will take. Even the changes you want to make must be personalized. Your Subconscious will respond quickly to the challenges that matter to you, but may rebel when told to accept what someone else thinks you *should* do. Stop smoking, but do it because your children are important to you, not because they want you to. Lose weight, but not to counter what everybody thinks. Instead, focus on the internal feelings and physical freedoms that come with being in shape.

Napoleon Hill, the author of *Think and Grow Rich*, suggested that the sweetest sound to a person is the sound of his or her own name. The personal nature of the Subconscious is why. When writing your letter, speak in the present tense and think in terms of "I."

Be Precise

Vague concepts and sweeping generalities do little to arouse your Subconscious powerhouse. On the other hand, the right amount of details and specifics will instigate its drive. Choose one change you would like to make or a single specific issue that you wish to enhance or correct. What *one* behavior could you change that would make an enormous difference in your life? Break your race or game down and zero in on the areas that really matter. Since numbers have a great deal of influence on the Subconscious, include start dates, end dates, deadlines, race times, or dress sizes in your letter and focus on the step-by-step application of your strategy. Analyze your goals and determine the precise physical actions and mental and emotional resources you need to get the job done. Imagine you are sending the Subconscious a message about how to make a dream come true.

Be Real

It is well known that sincerity sells. But it is not just the salesman's passion for a product that persuades you to purchase. You are responding to the individual's integrity and authenticity. Your interactions with your Subconscious require that same clean feel. Trying to sell the idea that you are going to ace every tennis serve or always be enthusiastic won't make it past the Logic Gate.

Remember the Kansas Experiment (Chapter 31) where the paramedics used a communication procedure to help first-aid patients survive? The trauma patients were told "The worst is over," not "Everything is all right." This small turn of a phrase made it possible for this important idea to make it past the rational nature of the Thinking Mind. After all, if you are in need of an ambulance, there is a good likelihood that something is very wrong!

Offer the Subconscious information that doesn't buck reality or seem ridiculously out of reach. Avoid a quick rejection of your ideas by omitting phrases that include absolutes such as "always," "never," or "every time" (Chapter 33).

Involve the Imagination

When dealing with the Subconscious, the old adage, "One picture is worth a thousand words" is true. In the Intentional Daydreaming exercise (Chapters 26, 27) you used imagery and the Voice to manage the conversion of information and energy. Here you use the same process to add color and life to your message. Speak with a tone of authority and write with the expectation that *what* you are saying *will* actually happen.

Use the imagination to give the Subconscious a view of the larger picture. Fly like a bullet around the track or lift a barbell made of feathers. Experiment and discover which sounds, images, and metaphors get a rise out of you. If it is too much of a stretch to imagine yourself actually being a bullet, then use phrases that begin with "it feels like" and "it is as if." "It feels like the barbell is made of Styrofoam" or "I feel as if I am ten feet tall" will break down the opposition you may find waiting at the Logic Gate.

Spin Toward the Positive

Words are like seeds in the Subconscious. Don't plant bad ones. Lines such as "I will *not* be tense and uptight" will fire up the Subconscious, but not in the way you might want (Chapter 32). *All* words, positive or negative, produce images. Power words produce powerful images in the mind. Structure the information that you send to the Subconscious so that it is free of neutral words and negative concepts (Chapter 33).

A triathlete once wrote, "When I get off the bike my legs quickly stop cramping and I begin the run." We changed the phrase to "My legs recover quickly after the bike ride and I start my run strong and relaxed." She triumphantly finished the Hawaiian Ironman.

Add Emotion

To attract and stick in the Feeling Mind, information must at least have the emotional charge of a Hallmark card. You will know that your letter has hit the mark when you can feel an emotional spark each time you read it. Power words also provoke passion, and passion will always pull you through (Chapter 56). Pepper your three-paragraph piece with words like "brave, courageous, and true," and other words that bring out the best in you. When you approach your challenge, do you want to feel "not so bad" or would you rather be "energized, excited, or electrified?"

Focus on Action Not Ability

Potential is cheap. Unrealized talent is abundant. Really, almost everyone you know is dripping with possibility and swimming in potential. However, the *ability* to climb Mount Everest is one thing. Climbing the mountain is something else entirely. The Subconscious is impressed with action, not potential. In your dispatch to the Deeper Mind, affirm the actions that you will take and take it for granted that you have the ability. Forget "I will be able" or "I am going to" and make statements that begin with "I am," "I now feel," and "I will."

There are the seven guidelines for reaching and arousing the Deeper Mind. Refer to the annotated examples at the end of this section for further help on structuring your message in Subconscious form. Remember the power of doing it now (Chapter 59). Why not take a moment *right now* and jot down a quick outline of your dispatch to the Deeper Mind using these guidelines? You can always expand, amend, and refine your letter over time. The Subconscious is looking forward to hearing from you.

Personal Trademarks

CHAPTER | 78

Doctors Ernest and Josephine Hilgard have caused a lot of people pain. Working with Stanford University during the 1970's, this husband and wife team conducted extensive research on the subject of hypnosis and the relief of pain. To study pain you must cause pain. The Hilgards used water torture to make their subjects suffer. Hypnotized volunteers would place one arm in a vat of rapidly circulating ice-cold water while the researchers gave them suggestions for becoming insensitive to the discomfort. The therapist might suggest that the subject control the pain by turning off an imaginary series of switches in the brain or by imagining that they were off on a hike in the woods while their arm was immersed the near-freezing water.

In addition to finding hypnosis to be an effective intervention for relieving pain, the Hilgards discovered that the hypnotized volunteers maintained a great deal of control while they were in a trance. The subjects preferred to think of the therapists as "guides" and *often rejected the suggested imagery in favor of scenes that suited them better or ideas that they found more effective.* For example, when one young woman was told to imagine that her arm had been chemically anesthetized, she bypassed the suggestion and instead imagined herself as the Venus de Milo statue, *without an arm to hurt.* According to the Hilgards, she reported only a slight tingling in her shoulder!

What is in a name? Well, when you're dealing with the Subconscious, the answer is "quite a bit." Corporate slogans, book titles, and advertising headlines tell a whole story in just one line. Like radio jingles and logos, slogans and titles condense your experience down into just a few syllables, an image, or a single sound. While the Golden Arches logo directly conveys "hamburgers and fries," it also sends a message of speed and consistency. Fred's Hotdog Haven might look intriguing when you are passing through a strange town but, if you are in a hurry, McDonalds usually wins hands down. Contained in those two yellow arcs are every Happy Meal you have eaten, television commercial you have seen, or idea you have related to McDonalds, fast food, and clowns. It is the same with Nike, Ford, or Coke; each company wants to burn their brand into the memory banks of your Subconscious Mind. They know that each time you hear their slogan or see their logo, it triggers everything you already know about their position in the market and what they promise.

Once you have composed your letter to the Subconscious, it is time to do a little branding of your own. Your letter to the Subconscious Mind needs a powerful headline. Create a title that symbolizes the essence of your message in one word, an image, a simple phrase or sound. Like the message itself, your symbol should have personal meaning and evoke some emotion. Whether you are an athlete who chooses "To Toe the Line with the Best" or you are ramping up your sexuality with something like "Little Black Dress," your symbol is a magical password that opens the Logic Gate and allows the free flow of information and energy throughout the brain and body.

In Chapter 42 you learned to use a word-signal to help you instantly relax. Here you are learning to use a symbol to immediately access the Subconscious and coordinate the whole mind. When you finish your letter and find your headline, it is time for a trip to your internal post office to get your correspondence delivered.

Letters for Reference

CHAPTER | 79

If you wanted my help in making a change, facing a challenge, or reaching a goal, we would begin by condensing your dream or needs into one or two sentences. From these concentrated concepts, we would use the seven guidelines found in Chapter 77 to craft your short letter or script to the Subconscious. Once we had captured the essence of the perfect golf game, the positive outcome of the operation, or the power that comes from describing personal growth on paper, we would then create a title or symbol to encapsulate it. This is your assignment. Concentrate your goals in a short phrase of no more than a few sentences, write out your letter using the seven guidelines, and give it a title or symbol.

To help you in this endeavor, I have annotated two letters as examples. These letters were written by actual clients and played an integral role in catapulting both these individuals to levels of success *far* beyond what they consciously believed to be possible. If you take the time to think out, feel out, and write out your letter to the Subconscious, it will do the same for you.

THE AUDITION

Inspiring and clear and all in one sentence — Goal: To liberate my spirit and creative expression and to share it with others by performing on stage.

"Shining" ——————— Many layers of meaning

Precise — It is July 2nd. As I arrive for the audition, I look around and survey the theater. When I see the other people, the stage, the curtain, the rows of chairs, I know I am at home.

Very personal — I soak in all the positive, creative energy around me.

Power words — Because I am grounded and comfortable, I make eye contact with the other actors, smile, and genuinely feel excited and happy for everyone. — Emotional high road

Reality based — I have practiced long and hard for today and I am ready to "Shine."

Affirms action — As I step onto the stage, I am focused and con-fident.

Solid physical directives — My legs are sturdy beneath me and I feel grounded, solid, and strong. My breathing is easy and deep and my mouth is moist. When the music begins, it fills every part of my body with power. As I begin to sing, my voice is strong and filled with attitude. Music is in my soul and I share my spirit with the entire room. I stand tall and my posture is perfect. I sing with my entire body. I control my breathing and my voice rises up from my diaphragm. The notes slip off my tongue with a clear, crisp power.

Precise — During the dance audition, the choreography comes quickly and easily to me. I let go and I move with grace, attitude, and style.

I am dancing on a beam of light. —————— Involves the imagination

Combines — emotion and imagery

My spirit comes alive and my creative energy flows with playful abandon. I feel this delicious rush of energy as a powerful light shining out and filling the entire room.

I am shining like a beam of light. My voice, my body, and my spirit are free. I love this level of energy.

During the audition I perform in my zone and at my peak and creative spirit touches everyone in the room.

The ideas, images, emotions, and actions contained in this script are all symbolized in the phrase "Shining." —————————————— Ties everything back into the symbol

THE RACE

Clear target — Goal: To race the San Diego Marathon in 3:30 minutes and qualify for the Boston Marathon.

"Rolling Thunder"

Strong — emotional start

Ties the ideas — to a time

I love to run. I love to train. I love to compete. Because I train at the perfect intensity and fuel my body with nutrition-packed foods, on June 3rd, the day of the San Diego Marathon, I am in peak physical condition; my body is lean, my legs are strong, and my heart and — Reality based lungs work at their optimum. Because I have a strong mind and years of racing experience and accomplishments to draw on, I enter this event optimistic, focused, and ready to have some fun!

Excellent use of the Voice — From the sound of the starter's gun to the finish line, I am in control of my race! I run a smart, well-paced, relaxed race. I have the discipline to follow my racing strategy.

Precise physical directives — My strong legs have a short, fast stride and my feet turn over quickly. I keep my feet close to the ground, my back upright, and my arm swing is small and straightforward. My hamstrings and calf muscles are loose and relaxed. As I relax into perfect form, my body's excellent positioning propels me forward. I feel like — Powerful imagery a puppet on a string, floating along above my powerful legs. I am confident, focused, and competitive.

Reality based — I quickly rebound from any difficulty and come back stronger and faster. I invest my energy wisely and use the lay of the course to my advantage. [Race times/strategy here] — Important details

Very personal — I am thankful and happy to be running another marathon and to have the gift of running in my life. Racing is an exciting, energizing, and enriching experience. I learn from every race and I finish the San Diego Marathon feeling pleased and satisfied with my performance. Affirms action — I choose to run. I choose to compete. All the excitement, power, and greatness that I find in running and racing are symbolized in the phrase, "Rolling Thunder."

Breakfast for Champions

CHAPTER | 80

Before rising from his comfortable bed and warm blankets, American author and philosopher Henry David Thoreau liked to start the day with a short motivational speech. Thoreau told himself that life was fascinating, people trusted him, he was healthy, he had an alert mind, and the future was bright. Stepping out of bed, Thoreau stepped into a world that was filled with possibility and great people. Thoreau may not have known it, but his pithy morning pep talk was making its way directly into his Subconscious Mind.

When you sleep at night, your Unconscious side is in charge. As you wake up, control is transferred to your Conscious Mind and the Logic Gate comes online. However, this shift change isn't instantaneous. It takes time for the Logic Gate and Conscious Mind to come up to full power. While the length of time it takes to transfer this control differs for everyone, each morning a doorway to everyone's Deeper Mind is wide open. Have you ever had a dream that was vivid and clear when you first woke up but vanished from your mind before breakfast was done? When you were conscious of the dream, but not fully awake, you were in what psychologists call the hypnopompic state. As the Logic Gate became fully operational, the Subconscious was hidden from your view and information about the dream was lost.

This open doorway to the Deeper Mind also explains why non-morning people can be so grumpy while their bright-eyed and bushy-tailed counterparts wake up so happy. Until the Logic Gate comes up to full power, your Feeling Mind is close to the surface and under very little restraint from your thinking side. Consequently, emotions have a tendency to flare or flow very easily.

The hypnopompic state has a nighttime twin known as the hypnagogic. Where the former leads you away from sleep into waking Consciousness, the latter leads from wakefulness to unconscious sleep. Once again, as the power shifts from Conscious control to Unconscious process, the doorway to the Deeper Mind swings open. Why are these near-sleep states so important? They are your ticket past the Logic Gate and into the Subconscious. *The hypnopompic and hypnagogic are two times during your day when your brain and body naturally enter hypnosis.*

Hypnosis comes from a Greek word that means sleep. However, sleep is a processing state, not an input state. Beyond the senses that maintain vigilance in case of an emergency, you do not take in information when you are sound asleep. Sleep is not hypnosis. On the other hand, near-sleep states are very hypnotic. When you are near sleep, your nervous system and Deeper Mind are liberated from the interference of the Logic Gate and open and receptive to input, just as they are when you are in hypnosis. The hypnopompic and hypnagogic are the simplest shortcuts to self-mastery you can take.

Unfortunately, most people use these important times of the day to complain, worry, and focus on the things they cannot control. The negative predictions and pronouncements you make first thing in the morning work like negative suggestions, creating really poor Transduction all day long. Likewise, focusing on negative thoughts or the information from the 10 o'clock news imbeds these ideas directly into your Subconscious where they shape your world view.

Tonight you will go to sleep and pass through natural hypnosis. Tomorrow you'll awaken and again pass through this important state. How you use this time will make a difference in your life. Since waking, sleeping, and natural hypnosis are inevitable, the real question is, "What kind of difference do you want to make?"

Go confidently in your dreams. Live the life you have imagined.
—HENRY DAVID THOREAU—

Bedtime Stories

CHAPTER | 81

Tonight you are going to get lucky. Right before you go to bed, pull out that letter to the Subconscious you have been writing and read it to yourself, *out loud*. While your family and friends may think you have "lost it," the act of visually reading the words, vocalizing the sounds, and hearing your voice force the Subconscious and nervous system to become involved. If you find it is inappropriate or too embarrassing to read your script out loud, read it silently.

Read carefully and make each word count. Even in silent reading, use the Voice (Chapter 28). How you speak to your Subconscious depends on your personal preference; however, it is best to leave whining, threatening, and bargaining out of the mix. Let your tone carry an undercurrent of energy, warmth, and authority whether you speak with the enthusiasm of a coach or with the gentle, loving interest of a trusted advisor. Most important, speak with the expectation that *what* you are saying *will* actually happen.

After you have read your script, get into bed and focus your attention on your letter's symbolic title (Chapter 78). *Make no effort to remember what you have written; just focus on your symbol.* As you do, images, ideas, and feelings that are related to your message will begin to flood your mind. You loaded the program by reading the script. You let it play when you think of the symbol. As your Subconscious comes to meet you at the threshold of sleep, it connects with the symbol and all it represents. Message delivered, you drift off into the sleep state and let the Subconscious take it from there.

In the morning, start your day the way Henry David Thoreau did so many years ago. Take a few moments *before* getting out of bed and focus on the headline of your letter. At first, make no conscious effort, simply allow yourself to connect with what the symbol represents. As your Conscious Mind becomes more active, read your letter again. Be creative; plan ways to integrate the actions that you have written about into your upcoming day. Let these powerful ideas, images, and emotions energize you and create a sense of forward momentum. Go to work, go play, go live your life, and trust your Subconscious to produce.

The Coffee Break

CHAPTER | 82

If Dr. Ernest Rossi is right, sometime in the next ninety minutes you will go into hypnosis. According to Rossi, a respected pioneer in the field of mind-body healing, feeling drowsy or blankly staring off into space at certain intervals in your day isn't fatigue. Instead, these momentary power outages are part of an important cycle that is regulating the way your brain and body function. Rossi says that these cycles, called Ultradian Rhythms, were first discovered when researchers started mapping the changes that took place between the left and right sides of the brain.

In the 50's, sleep scientists found that most people experience a period of dreaming about every ninety minutes. Known as REM sleep, this dream period coincides with a power shift that happens between the hemispheres of gray matter in your head. Later research determined that a daytime shift in right- or left-brain dominance affected the way people performed and altered their attitude. *These daytime shifts also came in ninety-minute intervals.*

Whether or not you slip into a trance every hour and a half is still up for review, but the next time you are feeling a little spacey, you might wait before you throw back that cup of coffee or wolf down that candy bar. During those times of the day when your thinking becomes diffused and your body wants to be still, *you are entering another near-sleep state.* Whether fluctuations in body temperature, blood sugar levels, or Ultradian Rhythms might be to blame, you have an opportunity to reach the Deeper Mind all the same. This time is special because, like the moments just before sleep and just after waking, you are aware enough to interact with the Subconscious without interference from the reasoning process. And you already have the tools to put this near-sleep state to use.

The next time you feel that afternoon mental fugue setting in, pause to send a message to your Subconscious. Before you ply your body with stimulants, take a moment and relax (Chapters 39, 40, 41). Once you have released tension from the body, guide your mind to your symbol and spend a few minutes letting the images regarding your goals come and go. That is it; relax, think your symbol, and drift along in your Intentional Daydream. Then, let the energy naturally flow back in your Conscious Mind and bring you up to full awareness.

The entire process can take less than a minute and can often restore a refreshing balance to the brain and body. You may still want that cup of coffee or even need an afternoon snack but integrating some dreamtime into these moments of daily down time is another easy way to get around the Logic Gate and deliver your letter to the Deeper Mind.

Back In the Imagymnasium

CHAPTER | 83

Baseball great and stand-up philosopher Yogi Berra once asked, "How can you think and hit at the same time?" The answer to that is, "not very well." You would be hard pressed to solve an intricate math problem while dancing the fox trot or to recite the names of all the fifty states from memory while making love. Physical activity such as working out, playing a sport, running, walking, and sex all require your Conscious critical functions to release control, and then allow your Subconscious Mind to come forward and run the show. This emergence of the Feeling Mind is one reason why sports and sex are charged with so much emotion.

In order to perform, energy must move from the top of your brain down into the muscles, organs, and nervous system to make the action or movement happen. Even though you are not in a near-sleep state, the energy still shifts from Conscious thinking to Subconscious process and, once again, the gateway to the Deeper Mind swings open. *In this "workout state," you are able to reach the Subconscious by going through the body*. So, it is time to return to the Imagymnasium (Chapter 52), but this time armed with your written message to the Subconscious.

Before you start your workout or prior to game time, preload the information into your Deeper Mind by reading your message out loud. Then put your message away and begin your routine or start to play. Focus on what you are doing and remain involved in the activity, but keep your symbol in the back of your mind. Think or silently repeat your letter's title and use the images and emotions your symbol generates to power your workout or refine your play.

The workout state is an easy access point to the Deeper Mind because it coordinates your intention with the parts of you that makes things happen. Even if your message to the Subconscious has nothing to do with physical activity or sport, your goals and dreams are working their way into the action centers of the nervous system all the same. Fixed ideas about habit, personality, or happiness can undergo a sea change when you integrate new concepts directly into mind and body through activity.

Take a tip from Coach Yogi Berra. When Yankee batter Ken Boswell came to Berra and complained, "I'm in a rut. I can't break myself of the habit of swinging up at the ball!" Yogi gave him this sage advice, "Try swinging down." Boswell's energy kept flowing out of his body and up into his brain, to power his critical process and run the Logic Gate. Yogi was right—Ken needed to get back into his body and focus his attention on two words, "swing down."

The Butler Didn't Do It

CHAPTER | 84

One son turned out to be a nondrinker. The other son was a drunk. Both had grown up with an alcoholic father. When asked why he became a teetotaler, the first son replied, "With a father like mine, what would you expect?" When the heavy drinker was asked the same question he answered, "With a father like mine, what would you expect?"

After all that I have said about fixed ideas, authority figures, and the power of Subconscious programs, I want to make two points perfectly clear. First, *no matter what has happened to you in the past, you are responsible for what you do today*. Your life experiences are the karmic cards you were dealt. Authority figures in your past acted the way they did based on how well they could manage the Mind Rules.

Parents, teachers, and police officers that manage information and energy well tend to understand that their words and deeds carry power and they use that power wisely. Political leaders, bosses, and managers who have found a way to harmonize the fixed ideas in their minds know that they can make a difference and they do. Authority figures who haven't learned to manage their energy often melt down precisely when they are needed most. Underestimating their power, they hurt or hamper people through their words and deeds and waste energy fighting demons that no one else can see. Whether the actions of these authorities are right and just, or childish and mean, depends on how *they* use the Rules. Whether their actions have a positive or negative effect on your life depends on how *you* use the Rules.

The same holds true for all the events that happen to you. Research has conclusively proven that stress does not kill. In fact, stress in controllable amounts is actually good for your mind and body. It is your response to stress and the way you use the Rules that makes the difference. Of course, it is hurtful to be neglected, to be abused, or to lose someone you love, but there comes a time to real-ize that the painful things that have happened to you in the past are actually...in the past. Once you have grieved enough over your mis-fortune, it is time to move on. How will you do that? By using the Mind Rules wisely. Imagine that the scars you carry from the past are like creases in fine leather. They give you character.

Point number two is this: *Some fixed ideas held in the Deeper Mind cannot be removed, replaced, or changed.* These ideas come as stan-dard equipment to everyone that is issued a body. They are the information, energy, and attitudes that are held in the deepest part of your being, the Unconscious. You do not transform these ideas, they transform you. To truly harness the energy of the Second Mind Rule, there is one more thing for you to do: Open your eyes to the Inner Life.

> *Do what you can,*
> *with what you have,*
> *where you are.*
> —TEDDY ROOSEVELT—

The Inner Life

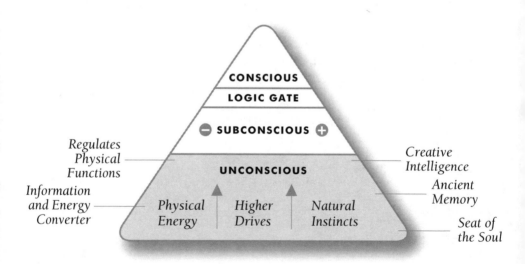

The T'ai Chi Tango

CHAPTER | 85

Neils Bohr was a party animal. One of the founding fathers of quantum mechanics, Bohr headed an institute in Copenhagen that attracted some of the youngest and brightest physicists in the world. Unlike his dreamy, aloof contemporary Albert Einstein, Bohr did his thinking with his mouth open. Work on theoretical physics was conducted across ping-pong tables and over beer steins at the Carlsberg brewery. Occasionally, Mickey Mouse cartoons were used to explain the latest theories regarding the basic structure of the universe. When a shocked visiting scientist asked if *disrespect* was a credo of the institute, a smiling Bohr replied, "Yes, and we don't even take disrespect seriously." So, when the Marx Brother of modern physics chose an ancient Chinese symbol to be the centerpiece of the Bohr coat of arms, no one raised an eyebrow.

Bohr picked the T'ai Chi because he felt it was the best symbolic representation of how the universe functioned. Since T'ai means "two" and Chi means "life force," Bohr was suggesting that the universe was formed through a *union* of opposites. In other words, light creates dark and hot makes cold possible. With its symmetrical arrangement of bright and dark elements and its suggestion of continuous cyclic motion, the T'ai Chi is also an excellent illustration of the balancing act going on between your Conscious Mind and the deepest part of your being, the Unconscious.

For the last thousand years, Western culture has become decidedly rational. Never before in the history of human development have the Conscious Mind and Logic Gate gotten to call the shots as they do today. Firmly in command and directed toward objectives, this

217

thinking consciousness has brought us the vast advances in medicine, technology, and lifestyle we enjoy in the new millennium. These extremely important acquisitions, however, have come at a price. All this attention to our Conscious intention and thinking has caused people to lose touch with the needs of the Feeling Mind and to fall out of step with the driving forces of the Unconscious. In the pursuit of status and science, basic needs like intimacy, equanimity, and adventure are being ignored. Worse, to society's industrious eye, higher human drives for meaning, self-expression, and wonder are not only considered archaic, they are viewed as flakey defects in a person's character.

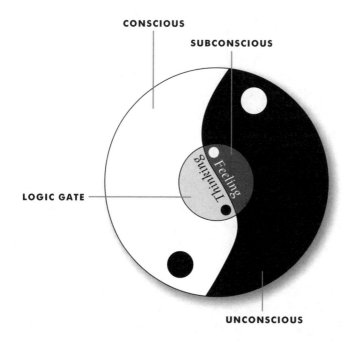

As the Conscious Mind and Logic Gate become control freaks and shut out the Subconscious and the Unconscious, the T'ai Chi of the mind is thrown out of balance. When the Conscious and Unconscious lose their equilibrium, people go wacky. What should be an awakening of wisdom and spirit becomes a midlife crisis, and men take out a second mortgage to buy a red Corvette. Lacking an outlet for inner creativity, people attempt to express themselves through shopping and seek their sense of wonder in an endless parade of movies, video games, and TV. Void of deeper meaning and blind to their own desires, leaders and priests betray the individuals, companies, or countries they set out to save. When people lose touch with the Unconscious, they tend to overcompensate for their feelings of emptiness and come to undervalue the gift of being alive.

The T'ai Chi Tango begins when you take the Unconscious into account and pay a little attention to the side of yourself that may be out of sight but is never out of mind. Dancing with these internal forces now keeps you from having to wrestle against them later. As the Taoist's symbol tells us, the key to life mastery lies in *unity*.

Unconscious or Ultraconscious

C H A P T E R | 86

Around the turn of the 20th century, the Grandfather of Psycho-therapy, Sigmund Freud, saw a demonstration of hypnosis that helped confirm his suspicions that there *was* an Unconscious Mind. A woman in a trance was told that she would open an umbrella once she was awakened and not know why. When she came out of hypnosis, she carried out the suggestion but could not explain her action. Freud concluded that there must be an unconscious mechanism at work.

Carl Jung also had a life experience that caused him to question what went on below the surface of the mind. Jung had a younger cousin who had gained local notoriety as a medium. While attending a series of her séances, Jung noticed his cousin spoke with two voices. In one voice, Jung could hear the intellect, interests, and wisdom of a fifteen-year-old girl. The other voice carried with it a depth of knowledge and a power of authority that was far beyond the young woman's non-séance capacity. It was this second voice that intrigued Jung.

Freud *reduced* the concept of the Unconscious down, finally coming to see it as a dangerous pool of primal energy that would wreak havoc if not consciously contained. In Freud's view, the Unconscious is a trash can filled with repressed information, sexual instinct, and need for gratification.

Jung *amplified* the view of the Unconscious to include a system that acted as an inner guiding principle and worked diligently to develop and expand the Conscious Mind. His theory of the Unconscious may come equipped with complexes and a sex drive, but it also points to a vast pool of knowledge that has been collecting in the brain and body over the eons and is passed down through the generations. To Jung, his cousin's ability to express a power and wisdom far beyond her years came from her inner *connection* to this vast, unconscious repository of collected information and energy.

Far from absurd mystical ramblings, Jung's theories about the Collective Unconscious make good evolutionary sense; the more conscious you are, the greater your chances of survival. Think about it, did you really come into this world as a blank slate? You had the instincts to suckle a breast, cry out to get your needs met, and smile. By two years of age you developed compassion and empathy for others, and from very early on you knew how to grieve. Is it so farfetched to imagine that a bank of inner wisdom is also guiding your creativity, intuition, and conscience? Wouldn't it serve the species well if the same survival instincts that keep you alive also *compelled* you to grow and excel?

To Freud, the Unconscious was a primitive pleasure-seeking entity that needed to be civilized by the ego. To Jung, the deeper side of the mind serves as a *mentor* to your Consciousness and constantly, although not always gently, guides you toward your greatest individual potential. Over the last twenty years, I have hypnotized thousands of people to help in their pursuit of achievement, growth, and excellence. Not once have I see Freud's vicious "Id" emerge. Instead, over and over, bidden and unbidden, the inner sage of Jung's Unconscious raised its mighty hand to help.

The seat of the soul
is where the inner world and outer world meet.
—NOVALIS 1798—

Tim's Dream

CHAPTER | 87

In Tim's dream, he is in a small boat on a raging river. Tim's boat is being swept toward a huge waterfall and he has no paddles to stop or to steer the vessel. People on the riverbanks are trying to throw ropes out to him so that he can be pulled to safety, but the ropes are too short or miss the boat. Tim is puzzled about the dream because even though he is in a very dangerous situation, he feels calm and O.K. When he asks me what all this means, I make a suggestion that he look inside himself for the interpretation. Managing his energy to change the way he is using his brain, Tim closes his eyes, takes a few deep breaths, relaxes, and smiles almost immediately. In the most clear and confident tone he says, "*I don't need to be rescued.*"

Carl Jung felt that dreams were letters from the Unconscious. Unfortunately, most people never take the time to read them. Dreams, visions, and even sense impressions are the ways that the Unconscious guides your Conscious along the path to wholeness, personal evolution, and power. Intuitive hits, gut feelings, and artistic inspiration are progress reports, forecasts, and solutions that point the way toward greater balance and unity in the mind. Dr. Jung saw this tendency for the Unconscious to mentor and motivate the Conscious so often in his clients that he even gave it a name; Jung called this trend the process of *individuation*.

As the word itself suggests, individuation is the process of becoming an individual. But there is more to individuation than just knowing how to make a fashion statement or singing the Sinatra standard, "My Way." Through individuation you align yourself with the vast experience and power found in the Unconscious and use that information and energy to live a life that is creative, meaningful, and very, very large. In addition to developing your uniqueness, individuation puts you in touch with remarkable resources and becomes the connecting link to life's big picture.

So how do you get on with this individuation process? You must develop a *working relationship* with your deeper nature. This means paying some attention to those guiding messages that keep showing up in your internal mailbox. So far, managing the Mind Rules and Information Transduction has been a viewed as a process for *sending* information to the Deeper Mind. This time your goal is to switch positions and get on the *receiving* end. Opening those letters from the Unconscious is the inner version of Information Management. Even if you do not reply, comply, or fully comprehend the meaning of the message, simply acknowledging your Inner Life builds empathy and forges a closer union between the two sides of your mind. Your *willingness* to pay attention to the symbols, images, and feelings that arise from your Unconscious encourages individuation and serves as your access point to power.

Once this open exchange is established, the next step is to decipher the important information coming up from your deeper nature and put it to use. Messages from the Unconscious are almost always encrypted in symbolic imagery because they are too large and have too many implications for mere words and concepts to contain or convey. Symbols can never be fully known by the limited and significantly smaller Conscious Mind. However, symbols can be *experienced* and in that way they become our teachers.

Inner Cinema Productions

CHAPTER | 88

Once asked if he had any advice for young filmmakers, the master of suspense, Alfred Hitchcock, replied, "Stay out of jail." This real-life incident is a good illustration of the humorous and often cryptic information that emerges from the Deeper Mind. Why are these symbols, metaphors, and images so difficult to interpret? The problem is the way information is processed by the Logic Gate.

Using the Logic Gate to grasp the meaning of an Unconscious message is like using a hammer to open a can of beans. Analyzing symbols that are nonrational and feeling based reduces their message down to a useless mess and actually blocks the meaning from your Conscious view. Think back to Tim's dream. To Tim's Thinking Mind, it was only common sense that a person trapped in a boat and about to go over a waterfall would be afraid but, within the larger meaning of his dream, that fact was only one small element. To grasp the significance of his dream, Tim had to move his Thinking Mind aside and experience the symbols without the limitation of logic getting in the way.

If you are going to participate actively in the individuation process, you will have to bypass the Logic Gate and use your *intuition* to understand and incorporate the symbols and impressions arising from your Unconscious side. Intuition is like thinking, feeling, and imagining squared. It is the only part of your Consciousness that is large enough to grasp the meaning of a symbol. As Carl Jung put it, "[intuition] is a *perception of the possibilities* inherent in a situation." The good news is that processing information in this synergistic or intuitive way isn't difficult, *if* you know how to intentionally open the Logic Gate or how to use the times of the day when natural hypnosis has you in its sway. The near-sleep states that take place in the morning and at night (Chapter 80) or the dreamy, diffused moments in your day (Chapter 82) are all excellent times to pick up Unconscious mail or process its more important messages.

However, you don't have to wait; you can create your opportunity to interface with the Unconscious by using Dynamic Relaxation (Chapter 41) or taking advantage of the workout state (Chapter 83). The symbols and images you encounter when you are near sleep, and the magic of intuition that takes place during your workout, will go a long way in helping you to unify the whole mind. The next few chapters will cover some unique ways you can encourage individuation by using those times when the Logic Gate is out to lunch, ready for a siesta, or when you can't think because you are too busy working up a sweat.

As you forge forward, please keep in mind that you are building a relationship and creating a partnership, *not solving a crime*. You are not a detective looking for the offenders in the Unconscious, and it is not productive to play the detached analyst. Messages from the Unconscious often come as a surprise and may not always say what you want to hear, but remember it is the *relationship* that is most important even if the information isn't always clear.

Wisdom²

If you were trying to cure a chronic illness, improve your mental health, or seek help in making an important decision in ancient Greece, it is likely that you would have made a stop at your local sleep temple. Named for the Greek god of sleep, Hypnus, these temples were the rage for anyone seeking a cure, looking to solve a problem, or wanting to kick off a quest during the 4th and 5th centuries.

With their elaborate exercises, meditation sessions, and hot purification baths, the sleep temples were like spas run by psychologists. The temple attendants chanted special incantations to help patients or seekers slip into a sleeplike state, allowing them to contact the healing god, Æsclepius. Æsclepius could work miracles in dreams. He offered signs that determined the course of action to follow, diagnosed the cause of illness, or gave clues as to a cure. This process was believed to rejuvenate the seeker's body, mind, and spirit and to awaken the individual's real self.

Flash forward a few thousand years to author and success scientist, Napoleon Hill. Commissioned by none other than steel giant Andrew Carnegie to document the science of making money, Hill wrote the monumental best seller, *Think and Grow Rich*. In a chapter entitled "The Thirteenth Step to Riches," Napoleon Hill talks about convening an inner counsel for problem solving and self-improvement. Just *before going to sleep* each night, Hill created an imaginary cabinet meeting between such notables as Abe Lincoln, Thomas Edison, and Ralph Waldo Emerson. Like the practitioners in the Greek temples, Hill consulted his imaginary advisors and came away with a wealth of knowledge that he put to use.

If you were an artist or photographer, would it be valuable to you to have a little one-on-one with Claude Monet or Ansel Adams? Maybe you would like take a private lesson from Arnold Palmer or receive some personal guidance from Buddha or Jesus or that long-departed parent. Perhaps you would like to visit an important upcoming event or spend time in a special place anywhere in your past or just have a moment to bend the ear of a wise imaginary friend. Opening the Logic Gate and interacting with the creative intelligence found in the Collective Unconscious can take you anywhere, granting you access to the immense wisdom that has accumulated in the Deeper Mind over the eons.

What does it take to sign up for singing lessons with Pavarotti? How about ten minutes of your time and a willingness to enter into a place of reverie and have a little repartee between your Conscious and Unconscious sides? I had a ten-minute "conversation" with Dr. Jung before starting this essay that was quite helpful.

Sometimes Carl is difficult to understand, with his thick Swiss accent and propensity to quote maxims in ancient languages, but he does offer practical and applicable advice. More important, he is always inspiring and encouraging, and I walk away from our little chats feeling more motivated and empowered. Now, I know that Dr. Jung died in 1961. I do not believe that I am actually talking to his spirit or his ghost. I am interacting with an amalgamation of everything I have learned and experienced related to the man and his work, as well as the vast body of information stored in my Deeper Mind. While all this may still be my interpretation of what the good doctor might say, it is most often exactly what *I need to hear*.

In every golfer there is an inner Tiger waiting with pointers on how to make a chip shot, and all public speakers carry an internal John F. Kennedy that can help them to create a powerhouse of a speech. When that larger body of innate knowledge merges with the infor-mation you have amassed from watching a player like Woods swing or hearing a speaker like JFK deliver an impassioned address, you access a level of understanding far beyond your regular mode of thinking or problem solving process.

The great news is that this deeper understanding can be *aimed* at your challenges and *charged* with resolving a conflict or building your dream. Like the ancient Greek seekers and students of Napoleon Hill, you can tap this vast repository of internal wisdom and modify its information to fit you and your unique situation. Every time you reach out to your deeper side, the very effort itself helps to build and solidify the relationship between your ego and your Deeper Nature. All that is necessary is your willingness to walk through the Logic Gate and play.

Ask And...

In this exercise, imagine you are a movie director who sets the scene and then stands back and lets the actors have the stage. Over-direction leads to wooden performances and predictable insights; just let the actors play. If you have been practicing Dynamic Relaxation, or use the Workout State, then you hold the key to pass through the Logic Gate and may start this exercise whenever you desire. If you are not proficient in relaxing your mind and body at will, or if you exercise about as often as Churchill, then simply wait for your next encounter with a near-sleep state. Before bed, just after waking up, or during one of those drowsy periods in your day, work with this exercise and tap the experience.

Start by making a conscious decision to contact the Deeper Mind and to get the most out of this exercise. Isolate one question or issue that you would like to address, and envision a person, place, or thing that you feel holds the answer. Where the Greeks were limited to their god of healing, Æsclepius, your inner guide could be anyone actual or invented, alive now or in the distant past. You could pick a relative, Julius Caesar, or the Great Pumpkin. Once you have your question or have identified the area you would like to explore, close your eyes, relax, and imagine you are opening the Logic Gate.

Once the information gate is open, imagine that you are standing in a room with two chairs or places to sit. Take one seat for yourself and put your guide in the other. Greet your guide and, when you are ready, ask your question. Exactly how your guide will answer is limited only by your imagination, and since the Subconscious speaks in symbols, *everything you encounter after you close your eyes has potential value*. One client of mine found the door was locked and he couldn't get in. Another went in the room only to find a note from his guide that contained his answer *and* an apology for not being able to deliver the message in person.

After you ask your question, allow the scene to change and flow according to the designs of your creative intelligence. Do not analyze the images or try to make something happen. If you feel that some symbol is significant, fine; get interactive and explore it. Ask further questions, participate, or take a closer look, but let the scene unfold. Stay tuned for the images and information that move you. When you find the symbols that hit you like a Hallmark card on steroids, pay attention! Images and ideals that activate your Feeling Mind or that generate energy in the body are important. When you feel finished, either exit the process by opening your eyes and going about your day or allow yourself to slip off into sleep.

What should you do with the information you bring back from your inner source? Call in the Thinking Mind and spend some time thinking about how to act (or not) on this information or how to best integrate it into your life. This focus of attention on the answers you receive from the Deeper Mind amplifies the process and strengthens the union between your Conscious and Unconscious sides.

You Better Free Your Mind Instead

CHAPTER | 91

Do you get some of your best ideas in the shower? Do the images in your dreams stick with you well into your day? Do flashes of insight flood your mind when you work out? Do you often sort things out while commuting to and from work? Do you ever wake up with a song, a memory, or a story in your mind? Another way to build a working relationship with the Unconscious is *observation*. Concealed in your everyday experience is a veritable smorgasbord of symbols, sense impressions, and emotions expressly designed to connect you with the energy of the Deeper Mind. That short fantasy you had about living in another time or falling in love with the perfect partner may be much more than mere wishful thinking. Hidden in these Walter Mitty daydreams are metaphors from the Unconscious and reflections of the ancient blueprints found there.

Childhood memories that just pop up, tearing up at some corny song on the radio, or even rapid mood shifts can carry with them an underlying message from the Deeper Mind and serve as an access point to power. Listen the next time you catch yourself absentmindedly whistling or humming a tune and ask, "Why that song now?" If you find yourself repeatedly panning over an image or reviewing a past event, don't dismiss it, delve into it. See if you can find a message in these memories or fantasies that relates to the events going on in your life today. Pay attention, ponder, and play with the images, songs, and storylines that just happen to cross your mind. Sometimes important information, strength, or simple comfort can be found in the smallest of things—a subtle gesture, a short poem, or even in a change in personal taste.

I regularly wake up each morning with a song running through my head. From "Take the A-Train" to "Zip-a-Dee-Doo-Dah," these tunes often, but not always, mirror my external experience and offer tantalizing clues as to what is unfolding in my inner life. For example, just before a relationship ended, I got up several mornings in a row with the words to Bob Dylan's "Don't Think Twice" playing loud and clear. Apparently, I was a little more angry than I thought. This was the start of a particularly dark time in my life. I lost *everything*, including my belief in myself. That is when this tendency to come up from sleep and find a song waiting saved me.

At the height of my decline, which happened over the Christmas holidays, I felt defeated and done. Then on New Year's morning, I woke up with The Beatles in my brain. It was the song "Revolution" and Lennon's lyrics, "You say you want a revolution, well, we all want to change the world" and "You know it's gonna' be all right" had the most profound effect on my attitude and energy level. For days those lyrics played over and over in my mind, and I was singing along. *While nothing outside me had changed, something internal had shifted.* I felt whole, strengthened, and feisty. That song was a signal flare marking the start of my internal revolution, and strength itself seemed to flow from those words. In this strange and wonderful experience, I had found the power I needed to get back in the race.

Ancient Blueprints

CHAPTER | 92

Gilgamesh was the world's first action hero. About 2500 B.C. in Persia, his story was carved into a series of stone tablets and the first media star was born. Gilgamesh had superhuman strength and a sidekick, named Enkidu. Together they traveled the countryside battling bad guys and having adventures. Like most action heroes, Gilgamesh had sex often and his personality got him into a lot of unnecessary trouble. A leader and a fighter, he was one of the original "warrior kings."

From the tales of brave Ulysses to the Knights of the Round Table, hero stories have been a staple in literature and mythology for many a millennium. Today, comic books have replaced stone tablets, Gilgamesh wears tights and is called Superman, and it is Indiana Jones chasing the Golden Fleece instead of Jason. While the characters and settings change, the story remains the same. A powerful figure with personal issues, a call to adventure, serious adversity, help from a mysterious stranger, romance — the same "movie" that has been showing for almost 5,000 years. Joseph Campbell dubbed this phenomenon the "Hero with A Thousand Faces."

So why do Luke Skywalker and Lancelot have so much in common? It seems that the hero's story is *imbedded* into our Unconscious, serving as an ancient blueprint for how to live. The hero's story is just one of many inner templates that come preinstalled in the Unconscious. These templates are the archetypes, the elemental models upon which our lives are built. In addition to the Warrior, there is the Wanderer, the Martyr, the Sage, and the Fool, to name just a few. These archetypes, or blueprints, can be found in myths scattered around the globe, and they offer a glimpse into the magnif-icent forces unfolding within and around all of us. Understanding these templates gives you clues to who you are, where you are going, and how to get there. They allow you to empathize with the Unconscious side of the mind and offer you an opportunity to live your life as a deep and rich experience. The archetypes explain why you are more than a mass of defense mechanisms out on holiday (Chapter 58).

It is the Martyr archetype that drives soldiers to throw themselves on hand grenades to save their comrades and that moves the young mother to sacrifice her needs for that of her child. The Warrior blue-print pushes mountain climbers to ascend to the roof of the world and propels baseball players into the World Series. Young minds that travel to find themselves are following in the footsteps of the Wanderer, and the role model for many teachers is the inner model of the Sage. Everyone knows a Rebel, and each of us has played the Fool. There are far too many of these internal models to describe in this short piece, but watch for the recurring themes that run through life and you will find an archetype staring back at you.

You can choose to live unconnected to the archetypes and build your life without consulting these inner blueprints, but do not expect these primary elements to leave you alone. *These internal stories are alive within you and they are looking to be played out.* When the story of Gilgamesh begins, he is already a king who has built the fabulous city of Uruk. He is swimming in wealth and sex, yet he is still restless and unsatisfied. It is this inner discontent that drives Gilgamesh out the door and on a collision course with adversity, high adventure, and growth.

The more critical reason dominates, the more impoverished
life becomes; but the more of the unconscious
and the myth we are capable of making conscious,
the more of life we integrate.
—CARL JUNG—

Is It Bigger Than A Breadbox?

CHAPTER | 93

One of the most popular television game shows of the 1950's and 1960's was a program called *What's My Line?* The game consisted of four panelists who tried to guess the unusual occupation of a contestant or identify a product that was associated with them. The panel could question the contestant about their profession but were given only "yes" or "no" answers in reply. The game ended when the panel correctly guessed the contestant's career or received ten "noes" in response to their efforts to root out the clues and divine the solution.

The highlight of the show was the mystery guest; the panel donned blindfolds and attempted to guess the identity of a celebrity. The mystery guest disguised his or her voice and also responded to the panel's questions with only "yes" or "no" answers. The program's climax was when a player guessed the famous person's identity or when the stumped panelists removed their blindfolds and beheld the mystery guest.

There is a similar game being played out between your Conscious and Unconscious sides. It is called "What's My Myth?" In this version, your Conscious Mind uses clues to find the answer to life's important questions, such as "Where do I come from?" "What was I born to do?" and "What is most important to me?" The mystery guest on "What's My Myth?" is the Unconscious ancient blueprint that is active in your life. To win this game, a host of your inner panelists must attempt to identify the archetype by discovering the underlining themes and storylines that are driving you. Recognizing these ancient blueprints and understanding how they combine with your unique life experience to create your individualized mythology endows you with remarkable power. However, like all stories, your personal mythology has two sides.

When warriors are at their best, they are the defenders of the weak and oppressed. When warriors are at their worst, they are bullies and mercenaries. Martyrs at their best are compassion incarnate. At their worst, martyrs are compulsive people-pleasers who literally give themselves away. Orphan stories can cause people to stand up for themselves or help them to justify their helplessness. Wanderers make great discoveries, but they are afraid of commitment and have a tendency to run away before the real work starts. Understanding the blueprints that are active in your life allows you to be aware of the pitfalls in your beliefs and to avoid the pratfalls that come with them. Divining the identity of your inner "mystery guest" aligns your awareness with the very core of your deeper being. Living your myth is the source of tremendous personal power.

How can you discover the personal mythologies that are becoming your life? Here are ten places to search for the underlying themes that define your personal storyline:

1. Your job

2. Your relationship with the opposite sex

3. The art pieces, plays, books, movies, and television shows that interest you

4. Your interplay with authority figures

5. Recurring daydreams or fantasies

6. Your hobbies, the sports you play, and the way you play them

7. Favorite sayings, quotations, historical figures, or stories

8. The manner in which you face confrontation, adversity, and hardship

9. Your relationship with friends and family

10. Topics and images that provoke a strong emotional response in you for no logical reason

> *History is the story of the ego of a civilization,*
> *while myth is the story of its soul.*
> —WILLIAM IRWIN THOMPSON—

Me and My Shadow

CHAPTER | 94

If you are looking for a prime example of mythology reborn as modern entertainment, it is hard to beat the *Star Wars* movie series. In one episode, the young hero, Luke Skywalker, learns that one of the villains he is fighting is actually his father. Skywalker's parental nemesis is none other than that interplanetary badass with a respiratory problem, Darth Vader. Vader is a menacing killer whose black helmet, black cape, and black mask make the fashion statement, "I'm evil." Luke's character, by contrast, has the demeanor and dress of a space-age Boy Scout. The fact that Darth is his daddy is hard for Luke to accept. The very idea that there might be a connection between them fills Skywalker with disgust and drives him into denial.

More than just great galactic soap opera, this segment of *Star Wars* points to an important issue in the relationship between your Conscious and Unconscious sides. Your internal universe isn't all hearts and flowers. Not all the concepts accumulated from prehistoric time and held in the Unconscious are pretty. Like it or not, there is a dark side within all of us, and we must deal with it. The same life-affirming force found in the deepest mind also causes the failing swimmer to drown his best friend while trying to save himself. The seven deadly sins come as part of the Unconscious package. We all have unacceptable impulses, shameful wishes, and dreadful fears that we would rather not face.

This is difficult and painful for most people to accept. Obsessed with perfection, or at least the need to be *seen* as perfect, they try to shove these dark elements down into the Unconscious, lock the Logic

Gate, and throw away the key. Unfortunately, rendering these impulses, notions, and images unconscious does not diminish their power. Instead, *the information and energy that is banished to the dark abyss of the Deeper Mind demands to be acted out.* Embarrassing slips of the tongue, flings of marital infidelity, and the horrors committed in the name of God and Country are all ways the shadow side overcomes the Logic Gate and makes an appearance in the outside world.

How do you deal with your inner Vader? The same way that you handle any darkness—shine a light. In this case, the light is the headlamp of your consciousness. Consciously recognizing and evaluating the dark information that occasionally rises up from the Unconscious transforms shameful secrets into a moral choice. Awareness of our evil twin puts us in a position to prevent or alter our behavior. As acceptance of our imperfections replaces sanctimonious denial of our shortcomings, Unconscious pressure is vented and the poisonous pools of energy collecting in the Deeper Mind dry up. When shining a light into the darkness of the Unconscious, it is best to remember the advice of Luke's teacher, the Jedi Master Yoda: "The only fear that you will find in there is the fear that you bring with you."

What Goes Up

CHAPTER | 95

Richard Alpert, Ph.D., was a research psychologist at Harvard until he "tuned in, turned on, and dropped out" and then met his guru. With guidance from this sage, Alpert became the spiritual teacher and humanitarian, Ram Dass.

Ram Dass tells a story about visiting a man who was confined to a mental hospital because he thought that he was Jesus Christ. Impeccably dressed in a three-piece suit, the hospital patient posed quite a contrast to Ram Dass, who had wild, shoulder-length hair and was clothed in the traditional robes of an Indian yogi. When the man questioned how it was that someone dressed like he was could be hospitalized while someone dressed like Ram Dass walked free, Richard Alpert replied, "You believe that you are Jesus. I believe that everyone is Jesus."

That philosophy works well when dealing with the Unconscious. Because of their immense power, connecting with the archetypes of the Deeper Mind can be a heady experience. High on this energy, the ego comes to assume that it *is* the archetypical blueprint and blows up like a helium balloon. As the ego inflates you lose touch with the ground, and the stage is set for a time in the future when your bubble bursts and you come crashing back down. Explore, play with, and connect to all the Unconscious power you can handle, but keep this is mind: *You are a part of something magnificent, you are NOT the source.* In the grand scheme of things, you *are* unique and special...just like everybody else.

The Whole Mind Is Greater Than the Sum of Its Parts

CHAPTER | 96

Charlie was an officer in the Office of Strategic Services (OSS) during World War II. As the predecessor to the CIA, the OSS served as the intelligence and spying arm of the U.S. Forces. Although Charlie never shared the details about the operations he was involved in, one got the distinct impression that his assignments were the underbelly of the already dirty business of war. These operations were carried out in the service of his country, to combat an enormous and growing evil, but the experiences never sat right with Charlie.

Like many returning veterans, he started drinking to ease his mind and turn off his memories. He drank until he was broke and living on the street. Destitute and desperate for some hooch, Charlie knocked on the door of a woman friend who made her living as a prostitute. When she opened the door and saw him, she tossed him a couple of dollars and said, "Get out of here, Charlie, you are ruining my reputation!" As Charlie was making his way to the liquor store, it suddenly occurred to him, "If she is a whore and I am ruining her reputation, then what am I!" As the Apostle Paul said in the Bible, "Be ye transformed in the twinkling of an eye." Charlie was. Charlie got sober and went on to help others, working first as a drug and alcohol counselor and minister and then as a therapist and meditation teacher. Happy and robust at seventy, Charlie looks fifty and has the energy of a twenty-year-old.

When your Conscious Mind and your Unconscious nature unite, magic happens. Carl Jung called this magic the Transcendent

Function. Along with the process of Individuation, the Transcendent Function is a fundamental building block in Jung's psychology. The good doctor felt that it was the therapist's job to assist the client's movement down the road to Individuation and to help clients to *bring on* the Transcendent Function. To facilitate the Transcendent Function, Jung encouraged his clients to pay attention to the information that came up from the Deeper Mind when they danced, made art, or had ideas come to them out of the blue, when they fantasized, during moments of reverie and, of course, when they dreamt. As Unconscious information makes it to the surface and on to the Conscious side, the balance to your inner T'ai Chi is restored. In this state of Conscious and Unconscious union and harmony, the possibilities and the power come together, and it is quite easy for a new you to be born.

The Mind Rules are life tools that help you accelerate Individuation and encourage the Transcendent Function. When the two sides of your internal T'ai Chi unite, life becomes charged with purpose and deep meaning. This base of powerful information leads to stunning Transduction, and you begin to live each moment in a super performance state. The apostle Paul was transformed from a Roman bounty hunter persecuting Christians to a deeply religious philosopher through a flash of insight. The convict at Auburn Penitentiary became a contributing member of society on hearing an offhand comment. Charlie was transformed from a broken warrior to a powerful force for good by recognizing a piece of irony.

When the tip of your Conscious awareness, the fixed ideas in your Subconscious, and the ancient blueprints in the Deepest Mind align, the Synergistic Self is born. But to dance with the Synergistic Self without stepping on its toes, you need to master the Rule of Power.

Be ye transformed through the renewing of your mind.
—PAUL, FORMERLY SAUL OF TARSUS—

Rule Number 1 and Rule Number 2

CHAPTER | 97

The first person I ever worked for had a sign over his desk that read:

Rule No. 1: The boss is always right.
Rule No. 2: If the boss is wrong, refer back to Rule No. 1.

That sign is probably the reason I have been an entrepreneur most of my life. On the other hand, its message is the truth when you are dealing with the Mind Rules. The First Mind Rule dealt with creating ideal performance states by managing the information that you hold in your mind and directing the energy that flows along your nervous system and out to your body. When all else fails, the Rule of Transduction will always pull you through.

Internalizing the concept "Where the mind goes, the body and emotions follow" gives you *immediate* access to greater self-mastery and personal power. No matter what challenge or situation you face, you will do it better when you have a handle on Transduction. Best of all, tapping into this important premise can be as easy as imagining a lemon (Chapter 2). Information is a universal mover and shaker. Master IT and you master your world. So, as the sign suggested, when in doubt, refer back to Rule Number 1.

The Second Mind Rule is no less powerful or important than its predecessor. The problem is one of size. While it is not very difficult to understand the idea that the whole mind is made up of different areas that work best when they work as a team, trying to grasp the workings of the Deeper Mind is like trying to come to terms with the number of stars in the sky. You know the universe is made up of billions and billions of stars, but infinity is too large a concept for the Conscious Mind to hold. In the same way, the sheer size and depth of the Unconscious is too large for your Consciousness to contain. However, just as every person has an intuitive understanding of the vastness of space, everyone seems to have an innate understanding of what these Unconscious systems are and why they're valuable.

The Second Mind Rule amplifies the First and frees you from having to rely on repetition to create change. Replacing or transcending the fixed ideas held in the Feeling Mind allows you to transform instantly at the very core of your being. In addition to creating indelible change, Rule Number 2 aligns your belief systems and allows you to march in step with life's larger heartbeat. If there is one truth I have learned over twenty years of helping others, it is this: *There is no real peace in life until you harmonize the conflicting ideas that you hold in your Subconscious Mind and build a solid relationship with your Unconscious side.*

Combining the Rule of Transduction with the Rule of Transformation paves the way for the Rule of Power and puts you in touch with the Synergistic Self.

THE RULE *of* POWER

"Control comes from letting go"

The Two Most Powerful Words

CHAPTER | 98

A Zen teacher once asked a group of American students, "What are the two most powerful words in the English language?" When one student said "one love," the teacher frowned. As another student suggested "no mind," the teacher sighed and stared at the floor. When the next student called out "enlightened compassion," the teacher feigned nausea and shouted, "No! The two most powerful words in the English language are, Let Go!"

Welcome to The Third Mind Rule, the Rule of Power. The Rule of Power simply states: "Control Comes from Letting Go."

While this short epigram may sound like a Zen paradox, it is actually a powerful rule based in bedrock. Self-mastery is not a tug of war between your Conscious and Unconscious sides. *In fact, the greater your Conscious effort, the less your Unconscious will respond.* The person who tries to stop blushing usually becomes redder. In the long run, radical dieters typically put on more weight than they lose. The man who tries to will an erection won't, and the woman who attempts to command her body to climax can't. You cannot force change or mastery any more than you can push a rope.

The Third Rule is one of the foundations of the 12-Step Program of Alcoholics Anonymous. (In fact, with slogans like "one day at a time," "higher power," and "easy does it," AA is a poster child for the power that comes from using all three Mind Rules). The concept of letting go is also central to almost every system of the martial arts. As Bruce Lee put it, "The less effort, the faster and more powerful you will be." In Buddhism, the Rule of Power is part of the Eightfold

Path, known as "right effort." Christianity points to this mental maxim when it says "Let go and let God." To our control-obsessed society, these concepts are as mysterious as a Zen koan and pose a direct challenge to the ego. In reality, the Third Rule is as simple as it is true. Instead of struggling to get a hold of yourself, the key to control is to let your self loose.

As we discussed in the last chapter, when you manage Information Transduction and unite the Conscious and Unconscious parts of the mind, a magnificent piece of internal alchemy takes place and the Synergistic Self is born. *This Synergistic Self is the natural byproduct of clear awareness, clean Transduction, and Unconscious collaboration.*

Since its energy is too large to be contained in your everyday ego, encounters with the Synergistic Self often feel magical or other-worldly. This larger-than-life connection accounts for the famed "peak experience" and creates that phenomenon known as beginners' luck. The Rule of Performance and the Rule of Transformation bring the Synergistic Self into being. The Rule of Power allows you to direct it.

> *I would liken it to a form of reverie*
> *[like] the insulated state a great musician*
> *achieves in a great performance.*
> *He is aware of where he is and what he is doing,*
> *but his mind is on playing his instrument*
> *with an internal sense of rightness.*
> —ARNOLD PALMER—

Riding a Donkey

CHAPTER | 99

Foyan (1067–1120), a Zen teacher of the Song dynasty, once questioned the mental state of people who "go looking for a donkey riding the donkey." The synergistic effect that creates the super-self can only take place inside of you; it cannot come from the outside. Teachers and systems can help cultivate the soil and plant the seeds, but in the end, it is you that must do the growing. Of course it is important to seek knowledge and learn from mentors, but remember that no matter how good the information you find may be, its power comes from the way you *process* it. The art of Letting Go is something you learn through use. Only your experience can teach you the wisdom of the Third Rule or help you to discover its remarkable power. Let go of dogma, rigid systems, and the search for the answer man. You do not need them.

Nor do you need to go beyond your everyday experience to take a walk on your synergistic side. Climbing Mount Everest or doing the laundry, in every moment of every day, in joy or in pain, you have the potential to bring forward this expanded version of yourself. *The Synergistic Self is a not a thing, an entity, or a place; it is the release of energy that comes when your Conscious and Unconscious minds coalesce rather than collide.* In fact, your awareness and participation work like a chemical catalyst that brings the Self into being. If Carl Jung is right, the Synergistic Self is actually searching for you.

Jung suggested that the very energy of life itself, as manifested in the organs, muscles, and nerves of your body, was diligently striving to create this synergistic event and to realize a greater potential.

Dr. Jung also felt that each and every human being had a duty to meet nature halfway and to lend some attention and effort to this grand endeavor. While you may have to find your own way to let go, the emergence of the Synergistic Self is a naturally occurring event, and that means that you were born with everything you need to create and meld with this high-energy state. Let go and trust what Foyan said, "You are the donkey!"

When knowledge and principle merge,
environment and mind unite.
It is like drinking water,
one spontaneously knows if it is hot or cold.
—ZEN WISDOM—

I'll Take One With Everything

CHAPTER | 100

In the comedy film *Caddyshack*, Chevy Chase plays an eccentric millionaire and master golfer, Ty Webb. Webb approaches golf as if it were a mystical art. He doesn't even keep score. Like a Zen monk in knickers, Ty reveals the secret to golfing perfection as, "Stop thinking. Let things happen. And *be* the ball."

Caddyshack may be loaded with high jinks and laughter, but no one is going to mistake it for highbrow humor. Interestingly, this popular parody shows just how widespread the concept of the Synergistic Self has become in modern mass consciousness. In today's America, the phrase "one with everything" has acquired a connotation outside the realm of hotdogs, burgers, and ice cream sundaes. While Ty Webb may be wacky, we know he is right; somehow control *does* come from letting go. Unfortunately, Ty never reveals his *method* for transforming into a small, spherical object to dominate the game.

Being told to be "one with the bike," "one with the wave," or "one with the rock" is a lot of "number two." When asked for a practical way to create a superior state of mind-body fusion, many teachers and professional practitioners are forced into spouting convoluted conundrums that sound a lot like "Be the ball." While metaphors may describe the feeling or the *experience* of the Synergistic Self, they miss the mark when it comes to relaying the brass tacks of how to achieve it. Twenty years ago I went looking for a *process* to set this synergistic energy in motion; what I found was ancient wisdom and a three-step formula for harnessing The Mind's Third Rule.

In Zen, a flute with no holes isn't a flute.
And a doughnut with no hole is a Danish.

—CHEVY CHASE—

253

Delete the Unessential

CHAPTER | 101

Before I launch into the next story, I have a confession to make. While I have proven to be a handy guy to have around in a fight, as a martial artist I am stunningly mediocre. I telegraph my intentions in neon and move with the fluid grace of a rusted tin man. By using my own story as a guide to the three steps of letting go, I am hoping you will understand that if the Mind Rules can help someone as inept as I am, they can help anyone at any level to achieve anything.

Our story opens on an informal practice session in the backyard of my instructor, Randy Lee. While I am normally, as I said, an average student, on this day I was close to pathetic. Randy was leading me through a series of punching drills. He stood facing me, wearing what looks like a thick flat baseball glove, called a "focus mitt." My goal was to strike the mitt with as much force as I could muster. My fists were floating through the air and hitting the focus mitt with all the power and intensity of a flying marshmallow. I was trying hard to put some power into my arms, physical tension was building, and frustration was setting in. Obviously, Transduction wasn't going my way. Being one of those gifted teachers who can teach even in silence, Randy was patiently letting me sort things through.

Sliding into position to release another punch, I relaxed my body and looked at the leather focus mitt. Instead of wanting to land a solid hit or visualizing the outcome, I simply looked into the face of the mitt. The circular grain in the dark brown leather caught my attention, and suddenly I was caught up in the sensory process of seeing. When the punch was released there was no desire to strike, no concern about success; I was just actively taking in the object in front of me. However, the satisfying thud of the focus mitt and the recoil of Randy's hand suggested a definite shift in power had taken place.

Again, as I moved into position to strike, I shrugged off my normal tendency to compare and evaluate my success, relaxed my body, and kept my attention on the leather glove floating in front of me. Details on the face of the mitt began to stand out and my perception of its three-dimensional surface took on a fascinating depth. Wham! There was an explosion! It was my fist slamming into the mitt. While it felt as if I was barely using any strength, the energy that was released surprised both the student and the instructor.

The next time as I slid into the strike zone, the conscious process of recognition and evaluation got the best of me; something was different and I felt "Hot!" My attention shifted from object to objective, and my next punch missed the glove entirely. However, as soon as I went back to studying the lines and grains on my target's leather face, the power and accuracy returned. The secret was, of course, E.S.P. No, not the Extra Sensory Perception that tells you that your Aunt Tilley is about to make an unannounced visit; the E.S.P. that I am referring to is the Enhanced Sensory Perception that you have been diligently practicing since Chapter 18.

When you focus your attention on the sense impressions in your immediate environment, without forming an opinion, you open the door for the Synergistic Self. Since you cannot stop thinking by thinking, you must give your Conscious Mind something else to do. The act of relaxing the muscles *draws* energy away from the top of your head and pulls it down into your body. Focusing your attention on your senses also pulls energy from these top-heavy, thinking systems and gives the Synergistic Self clear access to your sense perceptions. To me, the focus mitt was not ugly or pretty, old or new, or even an obstacle; it was simply rich with texture and detail. If I were busy evaluating the condition of the mitt or analyzing my performance, it would have drawn energy away from my body and diminished the power of the punch.

My experience in Randy's backyard became a powerful personal process. I began to integrate this movement of energy and E.S.P. into my life. On the speaker's platform, in the bedroom, and during long trail runs, each time I moved the energy from the top of my brain down into my body and centered my attention on my senses, the reward was consistently the same in that the Synergistic Self was willing to come out and play.

Ready, Set, Let Go

CHAPTER | 102

While Zen is famous for mind-bending riddles such as "What is the sound of one hand clapping?" its teachers can speak directly about the issues of higher performance and inner peace. For example, the 17th century Zen Master Manan wrote, "If you want to attain mastery of all truths, there is nothing better than concentration in activity." Nearly four centuries later, this was the wisdom that I found in the leather face of my opponent, the focus mitt. Exercises like Dynamic Relaxation, Enhanced Sensory Perception, and the Concentration Game made this discovery possible. Of course one must take the lessons, pay attention, and practice, practice, practice. But these internal workouts teach your brain to focus while they unify the mind. When that heightened concentration is put into action, the Synergistic Self comes on line. To cut through any difficulty, here are three steps to sharpen the sword of your mind.

READY

Before stepping out on stage, the world-famous magician, The Amazing Blackwell, would prepare himself by jumping up and down while shouting, "I love my audience! I love my audience! I love my audience!" If you understand the Mind Rules, it is easy to see the brilliance in this bizarre behavior. The problem with suggestions to stop thinking is that the harder you try to stop thinking, the more you find yourself thinking (Chapter 32). After all, thinking about not thinking is a thought. Accept this: You will never completely stop thinking. On some level, your mind will always be processing information and your instincts and defense mechanisms will be active as long as you are alive. The trick is not in trying to delete all thoughts, but rather to let them pass by.

The stop thinking solution is to give the Conscious Mind a job to do. *Put the Conscious Mind in charge of moving energy from the head down into the body.* Shifting power was what Blackwell was doing when he chanted "I love my audience!" and danced around. Others unconsciously try to move this energy by pacing, chattering, or taking large gulping breaths. However, if jumping around isn't an option and shaking like a leaf isn't an effective strategy, there is another way. Once again, the answer lies in relaxation.

Consciously letting go of the unnecessary tension in your muscles rapidly connects your brain to the world below your shoulders. Getting *ready* now becomes an easy ritual of taking in a breath and relaxing your muscles as you exhale. That's it. No positive visualization, no self-talk, just breathe in—exhale—and relax. When you can release physical tension in the face of mounting adversity, you are practicing the skills of self-mastery, not just paying them lip service.

How much you relax depends on your activity. Obviously, if you are about to step into the batter's box, total relaxation is going to put you face down on home plate. On the other hand, if you are in bed dealing with pain, then you want to get as close as you can to 100 percent relaxation. The point is to create the relaxed and ready state that leads to a free flow of energy and information and fits your situation (Chapter 41). In the steady release of tension, you will gain control over your breathing, increase your strength, and automatically find a more balanced position for your body. Once you feel the flow of energy moving into the body, there is a second assignment for the Conscious Mind.

SET

In the award-winning movie *Gladiator*, Russell Crowe portrays Maximus, a great general at the height of the Roman Empire. During the opening scene, we see the general, in the chaotic moments before a major battle, crouch down, pick up a handful of earth, and sift the soil through his fingertips while reveling in its fragrance. This earthy, pre-combat ritual mentally centers Maximus, who then charges into battle and on to victory. In the *set* stage, it is time to come to your senses.

As soon as you can feel the energy shift from your head down into your body, it is time to turn your attention outward (Chapter 17) and *set* your focus on the information streaming in from your senses. Use your Enhanced Sensory Perception and just become aware of seeing, touching, hearing, smelling, or tasting and let everything else go. No comparisons to others or to past performances, good or bad. No evaluations as to how well you are doing, either up or down. Let go of labeling. Let go of memories. Let go of predictions. For these few moments in time, just let go of all your opinions. Set your consciousness to work catching your attention when it strays off track and then returning your focus back to your senses. Let your sense impressions fill the place where your judgment normally sits, and then it is time to Let Go.

LET GO

The steps to synergy are like archery. Getting into your body, you draw back the string on the bow. Sharpening your concentration and focusing on here-and-now sensory information, you take aim. Now there is only one thing left to do—let go of the arrow. Go ahead: Swing at the ball, strike up the band, or start your speech. With your attention focused on your senses and your body loose and energized, you are no longer trying to move; you are just moving. Rather than rely on one-dimensional thinking, you are responding with all the knowledge that has accumulated in your lifetime as well as the wisdom held in your body and stored at your unconscious core. This foundation of information and energy is what golfer Arnold Palmer is referring to when he talks about playing golf with an internal sense of *rightness*. It is this intuitive sense of rightness that is your guide to higher performance, personal peace, and ultimate success. Now you're cooking with synergy.

The Cheerleader

CHAPTER | 103

One summer long ago, I worked as a professional window cleaner. My boss was a wonderful man named Bill Schulman. If you can picture a five-foot-tall walrus, smoking a cigar and delivering a punch line like Mel Brooks, you have an image of Mr. Schulman. Most of our work was with large plate glass windows in two- and three-story buildings. Since the buildings were too small to have permanent scaffolding and Bill was past his climbing days, I worked from a ladder most of the time.

Sometimes, when the climbing was particularly precarious, Mr. Schulman would ask, "Would you like me to stand at the bottom of the ladder?" He would then quickly add, "Of course there is nothing I can do if you fall, but it always makes you feel better to know that someone's standing at the bottom of the ladder."

When I help other people, I often feel like Bill Schulman. I can stand at the base of the ladder for the client, but I am not the one doing the climbing. Apart from a few decent strategies and a handful of good questions, it seems that the most helpful thing I can do is to introduce clients to their Deeper Mind and serve as an intermediary until their Conscious and Unconscious sides are better acquainted. In the times when I was successful in helping someone where others had tried and failed, the difference seemed to be a matter of trust rather than technique. I *expected* that if the client did the exercises and played by the Mind Rules, they would get results. I *trusted* the client's subconscious to get involved and come up with a solution.

"Rapport" is a French word that, translated into English, means both trust and *affinity*. Affinity literally means "a natural attraction or feeling of kinship." The first step in letting go of doubt is to extend trust and affinity to your unconscious side. While expectation alone won't win a tournament or help you lose weight, why not give your Synergistic Self some home court advantage? Even when the prognosis for a positive outcome doesn't look good, you must come to *expect* that, when the going gets tough, your deeper nature can and will get going.

While this may sound to some like the famous "fake it till you make it" philosophy, actually rapport is much more. Rapport is the real confidence that comes from knowing that the ego is not alone. This confidence is based in the understanding that magnificent inner forces are ready to spring to your aid whenever you choose to tackle life challenges with your Whole Mind. As expectation is transformed into experience, the trust and kinship between your awareness and the Synergistic Self automatically grows. Have you ever had someone you loved and respected take you by the hand, look you in the eye, and say, "I believe in you"? If you have been on the giving or receiving end of that scenario, then you understand the power of rapport.

Do Your Stuff

CHAPTER | 104

Dr. Milton Erickson was seventeen years old when he was stricken with polio. His case was so severe that he actually overheard the doctors telling his parents that their "boy would be dead by morning." Erickson was infuriated at the notion, and his anger fueled his determination to live. He not only lived, he went on to become a doctor himself, and the modern world's most influential hypnotist. Erickson's elegant psychiatric style and his innovative use of trance influenced therapists and physicians around the globe. His work gave birth to dozens of psychological techniques and self-help systems, including Neurolinguistic Programming. Even success guru Tony Robbins stands on the shoulders of Dr. Erickson.

Erickson learned how to help others through his battle with the pain and paralysis of polio. Intrigued that images and desires held in his mind caused his muscles to twitch, the young man began calling up childhood memories of climbing trees and running, in an effort to regain his ability to move. He taught himself relaxation as a way to increase his strength, and he focused his keen awareness on his toddler sister for tips on learning to walk. Unaided and equipped with only a meager rural education, Erickson, at seventeen years old, "discovered" the Mind Rules. *Eleven months later, Milton Erickson made a solo canoe trip of 1,200 miles.*

While he had recovered remarkably well, the damage from the polio forced him to live with a limp and considerable pain. One method that Erickson used to control his acute discomfort was to *transfer the responsibility for dealing with the pain to the Unconscious.* After all, it was the Unconscious that produced it! In describing one of his experiences with the process Erickson said, "The pain was pretty agonizing...so I went to bed with the intention of losing the pain. I didn't know how or when, but I knew that [the pain] would be lost. Then you leave it up to your unconscious...because you can't know how it is achieved without keeping the pain with you. When I came out [to the office], I suddenly realized that I didn't have the pain anymore." In other words, Erickson is saying that once you consciously know what you want to have happen, you set your intention and tell the Unconscious, "Do your stuff."

Kinship with the Unconscious entitles you to expect these types of personal victories. Pain control isn't the only process that you can delegate to the Deeper Mind. Any function that falls on the Unconscious side of the fence—performance issues, enhanced creativity, lowering blood pressure, healing, shifting emotional gears, or memory retrieval—can be turned over to the Deeper Mind for processing.

If it is that easy to get a response from the Unconscious Mind, why didn't I just tell you this in the first chapter? Well, because without some personal experience to back it up, this concept would have never made it past your Logic Gate. Dr. Erickson's unique situation of complete paralysis and near death forced him to develop a good deal of rapport with his Unconscious side. Before you can just let go and wield the power of the Unconscious, you must first forge a relationship with the Deeper Mind. To do that, you need a working understanding of the First and Second Mind Rules.

The Unconscious Ally

CHAPTER | 105

Paramedic and clinical psychologist Don Jacobs tells the story of a twenty-two-year-old bicyclist who suffered a severe cut to the scalp after a high-speed ride ended in a crash. Paramedics found the young biker conscious and coherent, but badly shaken up. His head wound was caked with dried blood, dirt, and road debris. Using his state of shock to get around the Logic Gate, the paramedics *encouraged* the patient to bleed just enough to cleanse the wound. The young cyclist, without any prior training or knowledge of how he was accomplishing it, turned on the flow of blood to the injury site! After the emergency personnel cleaned the wound with sterile gauze, they simply told the patient to stop the bleeding. Remarkably, the steady ooze of blood from the cut ceased and the paramedics went on to apply a bandage.

This amazing feat of mind/body mastery is brought to you courtesy of whole mind synergy. Shock, like exercise and near-sleep states, unlocks the Logic Gate and opens up a direct line to the Deeper Mind. Therefore, crisis and emergency, like the moments before sleep, just after waking up, and when you are out for a run, are excellent times to get the Unconscious to do its stuff. In the times when you need it the most, your Unconscious will be there for you, if you play by the Mind Rules. However, you don't have to wait for a fender bender to call in the Synergistic Self. Need to solve a problem, have a question, or want to improve something you do? Here is how.

Think the issue over for as long as you need to. Once the issue has gotten a full review, let go of searching for a Conscious solution and instead resolve to involve your Unconscious side. Set up some small ritual (Chapter 29) in your mind to put the ball into play. This ritual doesn't have to be complicated; it just has to say to the Unconscious, "Take it away." As you let go of processing information with the top of your head and turn over responsibility to your Deeper Mind, direct your attention to something physically challenging or routine and mundane. Run, bike, or swim. Clean the house, take a shower, or go for a drive. Sleep on it. Watch TV or shoot some hoops in the backyard. Go fishing. Go to work. Go into hypnosis. But let the issue go! If you catch yourself brooding or worrying about the outcome, stop and remind yourself that your Unconscious ally is also on the job.

With so many variables in your individual situation, is hard to say exactly when or how you will receive or see a response. Most likely, you'll find an answer or come up with a solution when you are ready to hear it or just when it is needed the most. Adopt an attitude of expectation and stay open to gut feelings, look for flashes of insight, and listen for the Voice. Sometimes this process is so automatic that the behavior changes or the feelings transform long before you become consciously aware that an internal shift has gone on. Sometimes the change is so deep that you only notice something is different when a friend or teacher points it out. Sometimes you get back far more than you ever dreamed or hoped.

The Monkey Trap

CHAPTER | 106

In India, they use an ingeniously simple device to catch monkeys. A small hole, just big enough for a monkey's open hand to fit into, is cut into one end of a coconut. The other end of the coconut is fastened to the base of a tree with a chain. The coconut is hollowed out and partially filled with grain. When the monkey puts his hand into the coconut to grab the grain, he can't pull it back out while it is closed around the booty. Because monkeys are notoriously greedy, they won't let go of the grain. Instead, they pull in vain against the chain and are easily caught.

As any parent with long hair or eyeglasses can tell you, one of the first motor skills a baby masters is grasping. This initial introduction to the power and pleasure of possession often leads to a lifetime where clutching, grasping, and clinging is the norm. Like many behaviors, what is cute in the innocent child is ridiculous in the adult. Needy people clutch on to others, selfish ones grasp much more than they need, and the rest of us cling to youth and opinion. Clinging is a natural instinct and even has a positive side. Needing others creates families. A great deal of good has been contributed to this world by ambitious, grasping people. Holding on dearly to youth and vitality causes people to exercise and eat right.

Like a rock climber, you must grasp the rock if you want to ascend, but hold on too tight and you will fatigue and seize up, never making it to the top. Just as in climbing: The tighter you clutch and cling to people, possessions, status, or situation, the more you increase fear and suffering and the less fun you will have. The balance point comes when you learn to live in the world and still know how to *let go*.

Luckily, you don't have to wait for your house to burn down or a divorce in order to find your letting-go groove. Prepare for these larger life issues by practicing with the Third Rule in your everyday experience. Let go of over-inflated or unrealistic expectations about what others owe you or what they should do. Let go of always having to have the biggest portion or all the best perks. Let go of having to always be right or getting in the last word. Catch yourself when you are overly concerned about what others think and let go of your need to project a perfect image. Notice when you feel superior to others or start measuring your self-worth by your net worth, and let go of that tiny persona too.

A meditation teacher used to greet his students with a hearty, "Hello and how are you today?" as they arrived for class. To the students who responded by saying that they were well, the teacher would smile and say "Good" and then move on to the next student. When a student said he or she was doing lousy or complained, the teacher would smile and say, "You are very attached," and then move on to the next student.

What's in your coconut?

Chinese Fingercuffs

C H A P T E R | 107

The look on my client's face tells me she is wondering, "What planet are you from?" Dealing with panic attacks hasn't been a picnic for this young lady, and it is turning her job as a waitress into a nightmare. Now, here I am telling her that, essentially, resistance is futile. Fighting with fear is like struggling with Chinese fingercuffs. Using your own energy against you, these diabolical finger restraints tighten when you try to pull your fingers apart. The harder you pull, the tighter the cuffs become. How do you free yourself from a pair of fingercuffs? Simple—stop struggling, relax, and gently work your fingers free.

As I explain all this to my client, she now looks like she has got it: I must be from Saturn. I go on to explain that the process does not require her to believe that it will work. However, the next time she senses a panic attack coming on, if she will let go of struggling and politely tell her panic to go ahead and have a field day, she might be surprised at the outcome. In the next session, the young lady is wide-eyed and more certain then ever that I am an alien. The day after our meeting, in the middle of the lunchtime rush, she had felt the panic building. When she told her fear to go for it, but she was too busy to go along, she instantly regained composure and, in her words, "all the power went out of my fear."

In a country where the best defense is a good offense, concepts such as allow, let, permit, consent, and surrender don't carry a lot of weight. While this go-with-the-flow idea may sound loony at first, its ancient truth is a plain fact: What we resist persists. Emotions are not directly controlled by will. Resistance only makes your fear stronger.

Why waste energy fighting a battle you cannot win? Let the individual who is concerned with blushing try to turn her face crimson. Tense before a competition? Fine, let your body do what it wants and tighten all your muscles for a minute or two before you attempt to relax. Nervous before giving a speech? Try to make a mistake in front of the audience. Try to shutter. Try to worry. Try to give up. Try to bring on your fear, your doubt, or even your pain, and you will find that the harder you try, the more difficult it becomes. This type of failing actually feels good.

Even in reverse, the Third Rule still applies; the greater the conscious effort becomes, the less the subconscious responds. If freeing your fingers from Chinese fingercuffs with this paradoxical approach is a bit too challenging for you, gain control by letting go. Stop struggling and tend to your Transduction. Stop struggling, send that letter to the Subconscious, and expect some core transformation to take place. Stop struggling and do something different. Stop struggling and let go. Stop struggling and realize that, sometimes, learning to fly feels exactly like falling.

The Letting-Go Limbo

CHAPTER | **108**

Each era adds to the collective vocabulary. The 1960's were no different. Along with bell-bottoms, peace signs, and sitars, the 60's gave the world wonderfully kinesthetic and visceral words like "groovy, cool, uptight." These physical expressions fit well when love was free and frenetic dance was the fashion. Well, it is time to "get down." While science may not know the exact mechanisms in the brain that allow you to let go, you can still train your nervous system *how* to do it. Admittedly, the Letting-Go Limbo is a little far out. However, this simple process is like mainlining personal power. I promise you will get "high," move in the "groove," and feel "out of sight."

All kidding aside, this is one of the most powerful exercises for managing energy that I know. Try it right now and see what I mean. The Letting-Go Limbo has only three rules. Rule one, do not hurt yourself. Rule two, do not hurt anyone else. Rule three, do not hurt the furnishings or damage the objects in your environment. Beyond that, it's your thing, baby.

LETTING-GO LIMBO

The question is not how low can you go or how wild can you get. The idea is to let the body take the lead and tell the brain where to go for a change.

Find any safe, open space where you are free to move around. Then, for just a minute or two, let go and let your body do whatever it wants to. Run around, jump up and down, twirl, shout, growl, or laugh. Dance, flap your arms like a bird, or squeak. Tense your arms, fall to the floor in a heap, open and shut your eyes quickly, or recite poetry while hopping on one foot. When it comes to this exercise, anything goes. Just move freely. Don't judge, just do. Once you stop your movement, take a moment to quietly scan your experience. Then go into action or resume the affairs of the day. Dancing the Letting Go-Limbo breaks up mind/body rigidity and allows internal communication to flow more freely. When done with true abandon, this exercise resets the mind and revitalizes the body in just seconds.

Think you might feel a little foolish or inhibited running in place, contorting your face, and humming a Motown tune? Good. Keep practicing until you lose that foolish feeling, and you will be training your nervous system to deal with the fear of criticism as well. Look at it this way: *If you can't surrender control when you want to, then you never really have control.* This exercise is a fast way to rev up the mind and body and bring the Synergistic Self immediately to the surface. Can you dig it?

Going Native

CHAPTER | 109

In the age when the sun never set on the British Empire, many English citizens living in far-off colonies clung desperately to the customs of their mother country. In fact, their rigid determination to maintain their traditional roles in these distant spots around the globe prompted Noel Coward to write his most popular song, about "mad dogs and Englishmen" who "go out in the midday sun." In the scorching heat of the Indian afternoon, or in the teeming jungles of Africa, the British colonists still drank hot tea and wore clothes that were fashionable, but far better suited to London's cooler climate. The English stuck to inflexible work schedules and read newspapers from home that were so old they were history lessons.

The colonists weren't just homesick, they were scared. The Victorians were afraid of going native. One day you start dressing more comfortably, and the next you are dancing naked in the moonlight to the pounding rhythm of drums. Inflexibly scorning their "savage" impulses in favor of more "civilized" behavior, the Victorians drove their instincts underground and their minds became a battlefield where the ego and the Unconscious waged war.

The lure of our collective primitive past is powerfully strong. This is the part of you that loves to feel the sand underneath your feet as you walk at the beach, goes gaga when you spot wildlife or catch a blazing sunset, and feels at home and alive when you hear rushing water in a mountain stream or listen to the wind in the trees. The need to connect with your natural side is the real reason that people still hunt and fish. If you do the math, the meat is almost always cheaper at the store. The same is true with the rise in outdoor recreation. Hunters and rock climbers may love the thrill, but talk with these folks and you find they are in it for more than just the adrenaline rush. It is this natural connection that gives a depth and dimension to outdoor sports and occupations and elevates those activities to the realm of the sacred.

The Synergistic Self is easy to find whenever you immerse yourself in the outdoors. No pagan dancing or ammunition is required. Just let go and walk on the ground in your bare feet once in a while. Make an appointment to go catch the moonrise. Notice the stars. Garden, walk, or go bobsledding, just get out and make some contact with the Earth! While you are there, use your awareness and attention and practice your E.S.P. (Chapters 17, 18). The rest will come naturally.

THE SAME OLD SONG AND DANCE

A student found Xuansha in the garden and said, "Master, I have come seeking the truth about Zen. Where can I access it?"

"Can you hear the mountain stream?" Xuansha questioned.

"Yes," the student replied.

"Then access it there," said Xuansha. And all was silent but the stream.

Don't Be There

CHAPTER | 110

A traveling swordsman stopped to practice in an open field just outside a rural village in Japan. Word traveled fast, and soon a group of villagers gathered to watch the master train. After a few hours the crowd dwindled down until eventually only one small boy was left watching. Wide-eyed and mouth gaping, the boy was transfixed by the power and grace of the swordsman's every move.

When the master had finished and sheathed his sword, he looked over at his awestruck audience of one and, in a curt Samurai tone, bellowed, "Yes?" The boy snapped to attention and said, "I, too, study the martial arts but no matter how much I train I could never defeat you. Your stroke is so powerful that it would slice me in half!" The old warrior bent low and put his leathery face next to the little boy's. Eyes gleaming and hiding a smile, the master said, "To defeat me there is only one thing you need to know: When my sword comes down to strike, *don't be there!*"

Some people play games and some games play people. From con men who consciously manipulate the pigeon, to your little cousin Kate, who unconsciously uses her cuteness, we all have a favorite game we play to get our way. You can change the way that you play your game. You can become more aware of what you do and how your game impacts the people around you. You can make adjustments. However, you cannot change the rules to other people's games or stop them from playing. Need games like "Drama Queen for a Day" or greed games such as "Winning Through Intimidation" are an energy drain for everyone, but people continue to play them because they lack other strategies for getting their needs met.

No matter what you do, until they discover a different method for getting their way, they will keep playing the same old game. Take the old Samurai's advice: Don't be there!

If the hysteria of the drama maven makes you hysterical, or the loud voice and angry words of the power monger provokes you to erupt, then it is *you* who is out of control. To regain your ground, it is time to call in the Third Rule and let go of your need to *participate*. Win the game by refusing to play.

Crisis on the part of someone else doesn't require you to panic in sympathy. Not every unfair rebuke needs a retort. The road-raged driver who signals with his middle finger, or the rude salesperson at the mall, are just bait waiting for you to bite. Let go of a past grudge and give up your fantasies of getting even. Let go of making excuses or personalizing every situation. Let go of responding hastily or quickly rising to your own defense. Instead, train yourself to observe and study your challenger.

Instead of getting sucked into the game, use your Enhanced Sensory Perception and focus your full attention on the person. Listen to the words they choose to use (Chapters 33, 34), study their facial expressions, body language, and gestures. *Come to understand the other person by watching them cycle through the process of Information Transduction.* Since most of the games that people play are childishly simple, it is easy to see through them once you get your own reactions out of the way. Recognizing how and when your adversary is going to strike, you can choose not to be there when the attack comes. Keen observation not only keeps you from getting sucked in; it will pacify the panicked, give bullies pause, and furnish you with the guidance you need to respond effectively.

You take this letting go process to a new level when you apply it to your own game. What strategies do you use to get your way? How are your games contributing to the games of others? What game would you be willing to let go of? The way that you manage information and energy when you encounter other people is a watermark of self-mastery.

Letting Go of the Little Picture

Time, Space, and the Synergistic Self

CHAPTER | 111

Physicists speak the language of mathematics to each other. They conduct research in statistics and post their results in equations. At some point, the experimenters may want to share their findings with the mathematically challenged or be published. To leap this communication hurdle, scientists must move away from the exact and consistent realm of numbers and signs and explain what took place in the laboratory through the inaccurate and ambiguous technology of words. Interestingly, the words that many physicists select to describe their theories sound like they should be coming from the mouth of Lau Tzu or Buddha. In fact, when you compare the modern physicists' description of reality to the vision of the universe held by spiritual sages down through the ages, they are often identical. Take, for example, the concurring explanations of absolute time and space.

Since the days of the Greeks, science has assumed that time and space were independent entities, which flowed on continuously and followed the laws of Euclidean geometry. Today, as physicist Mendel Sachs puts it, Einstein's Theory of Relativity has reduced the entire dimension of time-space to nothing more than *"the elements of language,* used by an observer to describe his environment." Buddha put it this way: "The past, the future, physical space, are nothing but names, forms of thought, and *words of common usage.*" While their approaches to making this discovery couldn't be further apart, for the scientist *and* the sage, time and space are the same: They are an interpretation of information! The way in which you perceive your place in time and space makes a difference in your life.

Realistically, your body must live where the mechanical laws of Newton have control. Gravity, entropy, and cause and effect all apply here in the material world. The problem is that life becomes heavy and rigid when you overidentify with mass. You become your body, you become your possessions, and the physical laws that limit mass, limit you. However, even if your body is trapped in the world of matter, your mind can travel in the dynamic universe of Albert Einstein.

Perceiving yourself as a system of energy interacting with energy is a powerful mind set. You are now free to let go of the fixed ideas (Chapters 65 through 69) about time and space that have accumulated in the Subconscious and that needlessly weigh you down. While identifying with a larger reality may not help you to levitate or walk through walls, these concepts can transmit a significant and satisfying sense of being centered in space and in rhythm with time. This inner sense of timing and balance leads to potent transduction, better performance, and greater personal power.

Expanding your perspective and stepping into the Synergistic Self doesn't take a doctorate in physics, and enlightenment is not required. You can begin to unshackle yourself from all that mass, break up rigid thinking, and start living in a more dynamic universe today, by practicing one of the next two exercises tonight.

In the history of human thinking,
the most fruitful developments
frequently take place at the points
where two different lines of thought meet.
—WERNER HEISENBERG—

The Final Frontier

CHAPTER | **112**

Morehei Uyeshiba was like the atom, tiny but mighty. Not an inch taller than five feet, the founder of Aikido could be attacked by a dozen men and end up tossing them around the room as if they were an army of helpless rag dolls. Film footage and creditable witnesses attest that Uyeshiba was able to do this well into his eighties. How could an old man have so much strength? According to Morehei Uyeshiba, his power didn't come from muscle, it came from harnessing the vital energy of the universe, a mysterious force known in Japan as Ki. Uyeshiba suggested that this force had the power to unite the world in peace and that anyone could tap this amazing resource.

The exercises in this and the next chapter are part of a series of internal processes, designed to expand your experience of time and space and help you to *identify* with the force that the grand master of Aikido was talking about. Please take them as guidelines that will prime the pump of your imagination. Once you grasp the idea of what the exercises are designed to do, it is quite likely that you find your own way of making this empowering experience happen. In the spirit of freedom and creativity, imagine this process is like learning a song—at first you sing along and then you go on to make up your own verse.

Like almost all of the Mind Tools, you can practice this process anywhere that it is safe and convenient, or you can take advantage of those times of natural hypnosis that occur throughout your day. The first exercise involves expanding space and instilling a sense of connectedness into your everyday perspective.

THOU ART THAT

You can practice this exercise in any comfortable position, standing, sitting, or lying down. Start by closing your eyes and focusing your concentration. If you know how to use the Rapid Relaxation process (Chapter 42), now is the time to do so. If not, any meditation technique or process that relaxes your body and quiets your mind will do.

Focus all your attention down to a place about one inch below your navel and fix your mind on one atom down in your lower abdomen. Imagine that one atom beginning to glow with a bright light. The light is vibrant, clear, and clean, and as you watch, its brightness grows. Soon the light touches a second atom and it too ignites with the same bright light. Now a chain reaction starts until the atoms set off the molecules near them and the bright light spreads from molecule to molecule until they turn on the light in a single cell.

As the cell starts to glow, it touches other cells and they too begin to radiate the light. As the cells start to glow, they spread the light to every muscle, fiber, and nerve in the body. Even the bones and skin begins to glow until you can imagine or experience yourself as a being of energy, radiating a wonderful, bright light. But the light doesn't stop there; instead, it begins to excite the atoms and molecules of anything your body touches. Soon the furniture that supports your body or the floor on which you stand begins to glow and resonate with the light. The energy continues to build.

Spreading throughout the room and moving along the ground, the light excites the energy in everything it touches until you, the furnishings, the room or space you are in are all connected and bathed in this bright light. The light continues to move outward, filling the building, spilling out on the street and into the other structures and cars and people in your city or town. Let the light expand outward until it fills your state and continues outward across the country and over the continent. Take your time and feel the energy as it grows and flows outward, upward, and onward from your position in space.

Imagine the light as it moves across and through the ocean and back on to land. Allow the light to encircle the globe until you, Earth, and all its oceans are connected by this bright and beautiful light. Imagine yourself as this bright ball rotating on its axis and revolving around the sun. Again, take your time and let this image sink in.

After a few moments, allow the light to expand outward in all directions through space. Imagine this luminescent energy setting off a celestial light show as it connects with each planet and star. And so, out from Earth the light goes. Engulfing the nine planets and the sun, the energy moves from the solar system out into the galaxy and beyond.

As one galaxy after another links together connected by this magnificent light, you notice one star drawing your attention toward it. As the light merges with this point in space, you realize that you are back to the atom in the middle of your abdomen and at the center of the universe. Relax and let this experience soak in for a moment. Now, wherever you are, you are standing at the center of the universe.

Time on My Side

CHAPTER | 113

One of the most common complaints people have about growing older is that time seems to fly by. Fine; then slow it down. When you live from holiday to holiday, mark time by the growth of your children, or send your mind traveling into the future for the majority of your day, time *seems* to pass faster. If you doubt that time is affected by attention, ask yourself how many more Christmases do you get? How many more summers of gardening will you have? How many more family reunions are coming to you? Twenty, thirty, even fifty are all pretty small numbers. Before you spiral down into a funk, please understand that, while you can calculate the exact number of seconds in a life, *each moment is timeless.* At least it can seem that way, thanks to relativity. To put it in Einstein's terms: "Sit on a hot stove for a minute and it will seem like an hour. Spend an hour with a pretty woman and it will seem like a minute."

The next exercise is designed to help you manage time, but you won't need your day planner or Palm Pilot. The time management you'll be doing is internal. Altering your perspective involves using your attention and imagination to slow down or speed up your experience of time. Similar to the World Stopping exercise from Chapter 48, this process helps you to find *your* rhythm and flow instead of being swept up in the rapidly moving, time-frenzied world around you. It is time to go.

NOW IS THE TIME

Find a comfortable space, relax in your own way, and imagine a clock face. Watch the hands as they go round, and now imagine them slowly slowing down until they come to a stop. Perhaps they are moving so slowly that it is impossible to tell.

Now, imagine that the numbers are fading and falling from the clock face. Falling off or fading out of sight. In your mind, imagine the activity all over the globe starting to slow down. The planes, cars, and people are moving at a gentler pace, and everything everywhere is moving more slowly at a smoother and more even pace.

Feel time slow down, even out, and move more smoothly. It is just as if you and the space you are in have slipped out of time's mainstream and become like a stationary rock in a flowing river. The current moves all around, but you remain in place. Your space is immune to the movement of time and you are on solid ground.

Use whatever images come naturally. Picture a falling leaf moving with the speed of cold molasses toward the ground. See sports played in slow motion. Imagine a cloud hanging motionless in an otherwise clear sky. As you start to feel your time sense slow down, activate your E.S.P. and step into the now. As you come to your senses, step back into the time flow but continue to move at your desired pace.

WHAT YOU CAN EXPECT

Taking control of your time experience is a great way to start a project or combat the overwhelming pressure of a deadline. You will still only get twenty-four hours in each day but, in your section of the universe, it will seem like so much more. As the pressure comes off, your productivity will rise. Practice before you train or compete in a sport and watch what happens to the timing of your game. I use this process to expand the time I spend with the people I love or the moments I am having fun. Tick-tock, it is time to reset your internal clock.

Head in the Clouds,
Feet on the Ground, Film at Eleven

C H A P T E R | 114

In the United States, size matters. Restaurant portions, motor vehicles, and TV screens all seem better when they are bigger. We are also suckers for glitz. If it explodes, lights up, and rings those bells and whistles, we love it (Chapter 15). Given our fascination with things large, shiny, and loud, it is not surprising to find that Americans confuse ego strength for ego size. Radio commentators and "shock jocks" blast their listeners with slogans and sophomoric humor in place of wisdom or wit. Magazines tout the personal lives and opinions of celebrities as if the survival of our species depends upon this knowledge. Reality TV is a nightly reminder that winning depends on what everyone else thinks. It is as if the whole world is still stuck in high school.

Worse, in today's race to be recognized and cash in on your fifteen minutes of fame, the gloves have come off and there are no rules. The aim of the game is simple: Whoever gets the most gratification wins. Unrestrained by traditional values and encouraged by smart marketing, possession and approval have become priority number one. In the new millennium, ego size is in the driver's seat and the damn thing has a credit card! However, I have come to praise the ego, not to bury it.

Unless you are going to live in a cave or join a monastery, you need the continuity, desire, and pride that a strong ego provides. Passionately wanting to achieve your goals and feeling triumphant when you do are important steps on the way to finding lasting peace. Knowing who you are and where you have come from, believing in your capabilities, recognizing what you want, and boldly reaching for your dreams *is* personal power. Physical pleasure, fun, and having the things you want in this world are all reasonable rewards for your hard work. Look at any leader and achiever, and you will see a tremendous ego staring back at you. Gandhi wrestled the entire nation of India away from the British with little more than his extra heavy-duty ego strength, a fact that never altered his ego size.

Enhancing your ego's fitness without expanding its girth is like watering a garden. Taking yourself too seriously and puffing up over praise, accomplishment, and possessions is like holding the garden hose straight up. The water is going to come crashing back on you. Sure enough, just as soon you start prancing about feeling entitled, grandiose, and giddy, you will say or do something embarrassing or something that compromises your coveted position. As political casualties Trent Lott and Howard Dean can attest, when you go over the top in public, there are consequences.

On the other hand, when you rebuff compliments and fail to internalize your achievements, you are holding the garden hose straight down. Now you have a muddy puddle forming at your feet. Playing the martyr and depreciating the ego is no way to build an alliance with your more surface side. *Success is supposed to give you a surge of energy.* Downplaying your strengths and victories causes you to squander this emotional upwelling and undermines your momentum.

Obviously, holding the hose straight up or pointing it straight down won't water the garden. The answer is the Golden Mean. Holding the hose out at the upper midpoint so that the water forms a high arc gets the garden wet. The key to dealing with the ego is to let go of extremes and follow the Golden Mean. Feel good about yourself, celebrate your achievements, but keep both your feet on solid ground.

> *Horse sense is the thing a horse has*
> *that keeps it from betting on people.*
> W. C. FIELDS

Why We Do It

CHAPTER | 115

What do your cousin's sinfully expensive wedding, the American Indian saying, "It is a good day to die," and a Norman Rockwell picture of the perfect Christmas morning have in common? Most human beings want to live in a poem. In other words, people everywhere seem driven to find the moments in time that are packed with significant experience. The desire to live the good life or visit an exotic land, like dying with honor on the battlefield, are all part of a deep inner drive to endow life with purpose and to capture its fullness.

Walking down the aisle with the perfect music and the perfect flowers, going to the family cabin in the summer, or climbing Mount Kilimanjaro are rituals people perform to transform life into poetry. People buy a multithousand-dollar wedding dress or inhale cocaine and party with friends because, for those few hours, they experience life as a poem. In those shining moments, they look to be defined and to feel alive. Of course, few individuals have a clue that it is this need for a larger life experience that is driving their behaviors; they take part in these activities with the notion that these manufactured moments will make them happy. The problem is that the poem isn't on the battlefield or at the altar; the poem takes place inside of you and largely depends on your world view.

The poem you find at Disneyland is the poem you brought with you on the airplane. The poem is in the sound of the afternoon rain as much as it is in a $250 bottle of champagne. When you play by the Mind Rules and bring out the Synergistic Self, you bring the poem into your everyday experience. Recognizing the moment-to-moment interplay of information and energy gives your life the dynamic quality that people look for in ceremonies and sporting events. Moreover, when you use your whole mind, your inner world and outer world *connect*. When you are in the poem, you feel a part of the main event and come to see your day-to-day participation as an ingredient in a larger, ongoing process.

Joseph Campbell was perhaps America's best-loved scholar. A masterful storyteller, Campbell brought the power of ancient mythology to life and rendered it accessible to millions of moderns. Professor Campbell once told a story about sitting in his Sixth Avenue apartment in New York City. He was reading an article about the Hero in Bushman mythology: the Praying Mantis. Feeling a sudden impulse, Campbell jumped up and opened the window. In addition to the traffic noise rising up from fourteen floors below, there, stepping onto the windowsill, was a giant praying mantis. Campbell said, "…he looked right at me and his face looked just like the Bushman's face. This gave me the creeps!"

On the exact opposite coast, at a completely different time, I am driving down Highway 58 in central California. Highway 58 is a rural winding ribbon of asphalt with rolling hills, open fields, and grand oak trees. The sunroof is open and it is a sunny, blue sky morning. Gliding through a series of S turns, I suddenly *know* that when I come around the next curve there will be a red tail hawk sitting on a telephone pole right next to the road. As I come around the corner, the bird is not only in the exact spot I expected it would be, but as I pass underneath, the hawk looks straight down through the open sunroof and right into my eyes. This gave me the creeps!

Before I go any further, let me make two points. First, outside of a few extraordinary exceptions, I have the psychic ability of your sofa. Second, seeing a hawk in rural California is hardly an unusual sight. That said, I will tell you that the spontaneous experience of knowing, coupled with our direct eye contact, made that moment magical and set the Synergistic Self free. In the early morning sun on that stretch of highway, I was driving in a poem.

Photo by Jim Little

In a series of interviews taped shortly before his death, Campbell said, "People say that what we're all seeking is the meaning of life. I don't think that's what we're really seeking. I think what we're seeking is an experience of being alive, so that the life experiences that we have on the physical plane will have resonances with those of our innermost being and reality...to see life as a poem and yourself as participating in a poem."

The poem for you may be the sound of your child's first words or the roar of the crowd at the Super Bowl. The poem maybe the sunset in your rear view mirror or carried on the tip of a French kiss. The poem is in your conversation with a friend and comes through that song on the radio. You may hear the poetry when you step onto the dance floor or as soon as the ball is in play. The poem is in the stars, waiting in your workout, and, hopefully, it leads you down the path of your career. The poem can leap from the pages of a book or ride in on a spouse's knowing look. The poem can come to you in your dreams or grab you with a sublime thunder clap. The poem is reaching out to you. Let it in.

The Last Waltz

CHAPTER | **116**

It is reported in the Acts of John that just before he was taken away, tried, and crucified, Jesus danced and sang with the Apostles. As they danced, Jesus made a series of powerful statements and declarations about his life and his place in the universe. Each time Jesus made a statement, the Apostles would sing out, "Amen!" (So be it!). Joseph Campbell called the "Jesus dance" "one of the most beautiful passages in the Christian tradition." Joining hands with his disciples, Jesus danced and sang and, in doing so, gave us all a very real way to face our greatest tests with the fullness of our being. I have no intention to offend. For the Passion to be meaningful, Christ had to *manage* his pain, fear, and trial with the limited resources of his human side.

Reading John's description, the parallels between the Jesus dance and an Olympic athlete warming up with the Mind Rules are very strong. Using physical movement to unlock the Logic Gate while making strong "I am" statements, *out loud*, in a powerful voice, sounds very much like the tools that a person managing information and energy might use. So, with all due respect, I suggest that the next time you want to bring out your very best, ask yourself, "What *would* Jesus do?" Then put on your dancing shoes.

In Chapters 11, 30, and 57, you were introduced to an exercise that involved an experience of energy. Originally the exercise was introduced as a way to focus your attention, bypass critical judgment, access your imagination, and manage information. In its second version, the exercise became a tool that gave you a physical sense of Energy Management and movement. In Chapter 57, you used this

291

same process to connect with the Feeling Mind and to amplify or reduce your levels of emotional energy. This time you will combine all three experiences into a single process that coordinates your nervous system and draws out the Synergistic Self. If you haven't been playing with this process on a regular basis, then take a moment and give Chapters 11, 30, and 57 a quick review.

THE ENERGY DANCE

Just as you practiced in the previous exercises, bring up the sensation of energy in between your hands and, once you have the feeling of energy flowing back and forth between your palms, compress it into a small ball about the size of a baseball and then let the force expand back out to a ball the size of a giant beach ball. Keep compressing and expanding the force until the energy in between your hands feels tangible.

As the energy builds, ebbs, or changes sensation, imagine the power of the universe filling the sphere. As the power intensifies, put your dreams, goals, and hopes into the ball. Imagine the task in front of you and add into the energy circle the physical and emotional resources you will need to accomplish these things. Activate your creative intelligence and let the images flow. Imagine yourself in the middle of your activity flawlessly executing your task with all the skill and power you need. Imagine yourself already on top of the mountain, receiving the winning trophy, or in some way achieving success. Put your dreams and needs and the passion that they inspire out into the oscillating and growing globe of energy.

Next, imagine that the images of your dreams and the energy of the universe are starting to bond. Feel the radiating power of this unity. Then, when you are ready, pull the ball inward and place all that power inside of you. Now just let go. Wait a few minutes and soak in the experience. Then, go for it.

Whoso danceth not, knoweth not what cometh to pass.
—JESUS OF NAZARETH—

Epilog

PROBLEMS — CHALLENGES — GIFTS

On October 4th, 1957, America got a wake-up call. It came in the form of *Sputnik*, the first artificial satellite to orbit the Earth. America's advanced technology and success inventing a nuclear bomb had made it the odds-on favorite to lead the way into outer space. Imagine this country's shock when the Soviets were the first to go "where no man has gone before". *Sputnik* was a problem.

More problems quickly followed. The Russians started showing off. Not only did they put several other satellites into orbit, they started shooting rockets at the moon. The *Lunik I* rocket missed its target entirely, but a second attempt scored a direct hit, becoming the first manmade object to land on the surface of another world. Then, two years to the day after *Sputnik* had roared off the launch pad, the Soviet Union sent *Lunik III* on a mission to the far side of the moon. For forty minutes, the craft sent back grainy black-and-white photos of the side of the moon that had never been seen by human eyes.

The Soviets topped this act by putting dogs in space in 1960, men in space in 1961, and a woman into orbit about the Earth in 1963. In the race for the final frontier, the United States was caught standing flatfooted. That is when John Fitzgerald Kennedy threw the gauntlet down. However, President Kennedy didn't challenge the Soviets, *he challenged his fellow countrymen.*

On September 12, 1962, in perhaps one of the greatest speeches in history, Kennedy told the scientists, politicians, teachers, and students assembled at Rice University, "We choose to go to the moon in this decade...because that goal will serve to organize and measure the best of our energies and skills, because the challenge is one we are willing to accept, one we are unwilling to postpone, and one which we intend to win." America responded to the call, and at 4:18 P.M. Eastern Standard Time on July 20th, 1969, Neil Armstrong became the first human to set foot on a heavenly body other than the Earth. The problem of Sputnik that became the challenge of President Kennedy soon bore great gifts. Communication and weather satellites that make life better and safer, remarkable advances in technology and medicine, and an upwelling of national confidence are all gifts that can be traced to the race for space.

From flat tires on the freeway to illness or old age, life will bring you problems. Once that happens, it is up to you to transform your difficulties into challenges. But the buck doesn't stop there—from these self-inflicted tests, you must come to recognize and willingly accept the profound gifts that emerge from this process, win, lose, or draw. This ability to harness the problem-challenge-gift merry-go-round is the trademark of all great achievers. All highly successful individuals are masters of converting problems into challenges and then reaping the benefits that come from the process—regardless of the outcome.

If you want be victorious in the game of life, you too must work some magic with the complications that come your way by transforming them into measurable and attainable goals, actively pursuing those goals, and then extracting the rewards waiting there. Luckily, you have the Mind Rules. The Rules are your tools now, tools that will help you harness the problem-challenge-gift conversion process and win. Trust them and put them to use. The Rules will work for you.

As you put this book down and go about your life, know this: Even if our paths should never cross and your name is unknown to me, I am pulling for you with all my heart. No matter the odds, the obstacles, or the adversity, no matter how great the challenge or dreadful the feeling of doubt, I believe you can succeed, you will succeed, and there is something you can do to create that success *right now*. What are you doing hanging around reading this book? Get going! I'll see you in *your* dreams.

About the Author

The essential secrets of life have always interested John Zulli, but it took an encounter in the martial arts to send him hunting for some definitive answers.

As a peace officer and departmental Defensive Tactics Instructor, John watched many of his students struggle with distraction, inhibition, and anxiety during training or in other high-stress situations. Frustrated that he had nothing tangible to offer these individuals, John began searching for a mind/body formula that could produce peak performance and greater power—on demand. What he found was The Mind Rules and what he was born to do.

Leaving his career in law enforcement, John began teaching the Rules to individuals, organizations, and teams. Within twenty-four months, he had established himself as a highly sought-after counselor, corporate trainer, and seminar leader, earning a six-figure income. For the next two decades, John used The Mind Rules to help thousands of people to break free of limiting beliefs and learn to live, work, and compete at their peak.

An innovative thinker with a knack for transforming unconventional ideas into practical life strategies, John's extraordinary speaking and teaching talent has touched the hearts and opened the minds of audiences worldwide.

John Zulli lives in sunny San Luis Obispo, California, where he is busy turning The Mind Rules into a unique series of books, CDs, and DVDs guaranteed to help you improve, change, and win.

References

Asimov, Isaac. *Chronology of Science and Discovery*. New York: Harper & Row, 1989.

Bercholz, Samuel, and Sherab Kohan. *An Introduction to The Buddha and His Teaching*. New York: Barnes & Noble, 1993.

Bloch, George. *Body & Self*. Los Altos, CA: William Kaufmann, 1985.

Campbell, Joseph. *The Portable Jung*. New York: Viking, 1971.

Capra, Fritjof. *The Tao of Physics*. Boston, MA: Shambhala, 1991.

Foyan. Translated by Thomas Cleary. *Instant Zen: Waking Up in the Present*. Berkeley, CA: North Atlantic, 1994.

Combs, Allan, and Mark Holland. *Synchronicity: Science, Myth, and the Trickster*. New York: Paragon House, 1990.

Corsini, Raymond. *Current Psychotherapies*. Itasca, IL: F.E. Peacock, 1984.

Corliss, William. *The Unfathomed Mind: A Handbook of Unusual Mental Phenomena*. Glen Arm, MD: Source Book, 1982.

Erickson, Milton, *Healing in Hypnosis: Volume I*. New York: Irvington, 1983.

Ferrucci, Piero. *What We May Be*. New York: Tarcher Putnam, 1982.

Frankl, Victor. *Man's Search for Meaning*. New York: Washington Square Press, 1963.

Hafen, B., et al. *Mind/Body Health: The Effects of Attitudes, Emotions, and Relationships*. Needham, MA: Allyn & Bacon, 1996.

Hamilton, Edith, *Mythology: Timeless Tales of Gods and Heroes*. Boston, MA: Mentor, 1969.

Hesse, Herman. *Siddhartha*. Minneola, NY: Dover, 1998.

Hilgard, Ernest, and Josephine Hilgard. *Hypnosis in the Relief of Pain*. Los Altos, CA: William Kaufmann, 1983.

Hill, Napoleon. *Think & Grow Rich*. New York: Ballantine, 1960.

Hopcke, Robert. *A Guide to the Collected Works of C.G. Jung*. Boston, MA: Shambhala, 1989.

Humbert, Elie. *C.G. Jung: The Fundamentals of Theory and Practice*. Wilmette, IL: Chiron, 1988.

Hyams, Joe. *Zen in the Martial Arts*. New York: Putnam, 1979.

Jacobs, Donald. *Patient Communication: The First Hour of Trauma*. Englewood Cliffs, NJ: Prentice Hall, 1991.

Krakauer, Jon. *Into Thin Air*. New York: First Anchor Books, 1997.

Lee, Bruce. *Tao of Jeet Kune Do*. Burbank, CA: Ohara, 1976.

Manchester, William. *The Last Lion*. New York: Dell, 1988.

March, Robert H. *Physics For Poets*. New York: McGraw-Hill, 1970.

Moyers, Bill. *Joseph Campbell: The Power of Myth with Bill Moyers*. New York: Doubleday, 1988.

Pearson, Carol. *The Hero Within: Six Archetypes We Live By*. New

York: Harper Collins, 1991.

Reynolds, David. *Constructive Living.* Hawaii: University of Hawaii Press, 1984.

Rossi, Ernest. *The Psychobiology of Mind-Body Healing.* New York: Norton, 1993.

Sanford, Rod. *Law Enforcement: Reasonable Force Options.* Soquel, CA: Pacific Institute of Defensive Tactics, 1998.

Shah, Idries. *The Pleasantries of the Incredible Mulla Nasrudin.* New York: Penguin, 1968.

Simpson, Joe. *Touching the Void.* New York: Harper & Row, 1989.

Tulku, Tarthang. *Time, Space and Knowledge: A New Vision of Reality.* Berkeley, CA: Dharma Press, 1977.

Williams, Jay. *The 24-Hour Turnaround: The Formula for Permanent Weight Loss, Anti-aging, and Optimal Health—Starting Today.* New York: Harper Collins, 2002.

Winokur, Jon. *Zen to Go.* New York: Plume, 1990.

Index

M

N

O

P

Q

questions, asking the right 84

R

Ram Dass 240

rapport 260

Rational Emotive Therapy 71

reactions, created by information
    11, 19

reality 36

relaxation

    dynamic 99

    exercises 97, 99, 102, 105

    and power 94

    real-world practice 105

    and sleep 114

    and tension 97

    and the Voice 102

    words as signals for 102

resisting, letting go of 268

responses

    to adversity 84

    automatic 90, 102

responsibility, taking 19

rest 111

"Richard Cory" 159

Robbins, Tony 10

Robinson, Edwin 159

Rossi, Ernest 210

Rumplestilskin 132

S

sample personal letters 202–205

Sanford, Rod 92, 93

Schulman, Bill 260

Second Rule

    defined 149

    and feelings 159

    and First Rule 243

    and information 152, 192

    and IT 192

    and writing 192

self-control and personal growth
    189

Selye, Hans 2

senses and apperception 181

sensory experiences, focusing on
    46, 48–49

September 11, 2001, and
    attention 40

Thank you for buying this book.
If you are interested in additional products especially
designed to help you live well and prosper,
please come visit my website:

www.themindrules.com

Or just stop by and let me know
what you think about the Rules.
I hope to hear from you.

NOTES

NOTES